OPPOSING VIEWPOINTS® SERIES

Uber, Lyft, Airbnb, and the Sharing Economy

Rachel Bozek, Book Editor

GREENHAVEN PUBLISHING

Published in 2018 by Greenhaven Publishing, LLC
353 3rd Avenue, Suite 255, New York, NY 10010

Articles in Greenhaven Publishing anthologies are often edited for length to meet page
requirements. In addition, original titles of these works are changed to clearly present
the main thesis and to explicitly indicate the author's opinion. Every effort is made to
ensure that Greenhaven Publishing accurately reflects the original intent of the authors.
Every effort has been made to trace the owners of the copyrighted material.

Cover image: Richard Levine/Alamy Stock Photo

Library of Congress Cataloging-in-Publication Data

Names: Bozek, Rachel, editor.
Title: Uber, Lyft, Airbnb, and the sharing economy / edited by Rachel Bozek.
Description: New York : Greenhaven Publishing, 2018. | Series: Opposing viewpoints
| Includes biographical references and index. | Audience: Grades 9-12.
Identifiers: LCCN ISBN 9781534500488 (library bound) | ISBN 9781534500464
(pbk.)
Subjects: LCSH: Cooperation. | Sharing—Economic aspects. | Economics—
Sociological aspects.
Classification: LCC HD2963.U247 2018 | DDC 339.47—dc23

Manufactured in the United States of America

Website: http://greenhavenpublishing.com

Uber, Lyft, Airbnb, and the Sharing Economy

Other Books of Related Interest

Opposing Viewpoints Series

Consumerism
Corporate Social Responsibility
Democracy
Deregulation
The Millennial Generation
Outsourcing
The Wealth Gap

At Issue Series

Corporate Corruption
Distracted Driving
Drunk Driving
Manufacturing Jobs in the U.S.
Transportation Infrastructure
What Are the Jobs of the Future?
What Is the Future of the U.S. Economy?

Current Controversies Series

Capitalism
Jobs in America
Mobile Apps
Privacy and Security in the Digital Age
The U.S. Economy
The Wage Gap
The World Economy

> "Congress shall make no law ... abridging the freedom of speech, or of the press."

First Amendment to the US Constitution

The basic foundation of our democracy is the First Amendment guarantee of freedom of expression. The Opposing Viewpoints series is dedicated to the concept of this basic freedom and the idea that it is more important to practice it than to enshrine it.

Contents

Chapter 1: Is the "Sharing Economy" Really About Sharing?

Chapter 2: How Do the Sharing Economy and Conventional Businesses Affect One Another?

The Importance of Opposing Viewpoints

Perhaps every generation experiences a period in time in which the populace seems especially polarized, starkly divided on the important issues of the day and gravitating toward the far ends of the political spectrum and away from a consensus-facilitating middle ground. The world that today's students are growing up in and that they will soon enter into as active and engaged citizens is deeply fragmented in just this way. Issues relating to terrorism, immigration, women's rights, minority rights, race relations, health care, taxation, wealth and poverty, the environment, policing, military intervention, the proper role of government—in some ways, perennial issues that are freshly and uniquely urgent and vital with each new generation—are currently roiling the world.

If we are to foster a knowledgeable, responsible, active, and engaged citizenry among today's youth, we must provide them with the intellectual, interpretive, and critical-thinking tools and experience necessary to make sense of the world around them and of the all-important debates and arguments that inform it. After all, the outcome of these debates will in large measure determine the future course, prospects, and outcomes of the world and its peoples, particularly its youth. If they are to become successful members of society and productive and informed citizens, students need to learn how to evaluate the strengths and weaknesses of someone else's arguments, how to sift fact from opinion and fallacy, and how to test the relative merits and validity of their own opinions against the known facts and the best possible available information. The landmark series Opposing Viewpoints has been providing students with just such critical-thinking skills and exposure to the debates surrounding society's most urgent contemporary issues for many years, and it continues to serve this essential role with undiminished commitment, care, and rigor.

The key to the series's success in achieving its goal of sharpening students' critical-thinking and analytic skills resides in its title—

Opposing Viewpoints. In every intriguing, compelling, and engaging volume of this series, readers are presented with the widest possible spectrum of distinct viewpoints, expert opinions, and informed argumentation and commentary, supplied by some of today's leading academics, thinkers, analysts, politicians, policy makers, economists, activists, change agents, and advocates. Every opinion and argument anthologized here is presented objectively and accorded respect. There is no editorializing in any introductory text or in the arrangement and order of the pieces. No piece is included as a "straw man," an easy ideological target for cheap point-scoring. As wide and inclusive a range of viewpoints as possible is offered, with no privileging of one particular political ideology or cultural perspective over another. It is left to each individual reader to evaluate the relative merits of each argument—as he or she sees it, and with the use of ever-growing critical-thinking skills—and grapple with his or her own assumptions, beliefs, and perspectives to determine how convincing or successful any given argument is and how the reader's own stance on the issue may be modified or altered in response to it.

This process is facilitated and supported by volume, chapter, and selection introductions that provide readers with the essential context they need to begin engaging with the spotlighted issues, with the debates surrounding them, and with their own perhaps shifting or nascent opinions on them. In addition, guided reading and discussion questions encourage readers to determine the authors' point of view and purpose, interrogate and analyze the various arguments and their rhetoric and structure, evaluate the arguments' strengths and weaknesses, test their claims against available facts and evidence, judge the validity of the reasoning, and bring into clearer, sharper focus the reader's own beliefs and conclusions and how they may differ from or align with those in the collection or those of their classmates.

Research has shown that reading comprehension skills improve dramatically when students are provided with compelling, intriguing, and relevant "discussable" texts. The subject matter of these collections could not be more compelling, intriguing, or urgently relevant to today's students and the world they are poised to inherit. The anthologized articles and the reading and discussion questions that are included with them also provide the basis for stimulating, lively, and passionate classroom debates. Students who are compelled to anticipate objections to their own argument and identify the flaws in those of an opponent read more carefully, think more critically, and steep themselves in relevant context, facts, and information more thoroughly. In short, using discussable text of the kind provided by every single volume in the Opposing Viewpoints series encourages close reading, facilitates reading comprehension, fosters research, strengthens critical thinking, and greatly enlivens and energizes classroom discussion and participation. The entire learning process is deepened, extended, and strengthened.

For all of these reasons, Opposing Viewpoints continues to be exactly the right resource at exactly the right time—when we most need to provide readers with the critical-thinking tools and skills that will not only serve them well in school but also in their careers and their daily lives as decision-making family members, community members, and citizens. This series encourages respectful engagement with and analysis of opposing viewpoints and fosters a resulting increase in the strength and rigor of one's own opinions and stances. As such, it helps make readers "future ready," and that readiness will pay rich dividends for the readers themselves, for the citizenry, for our society, and for the world at large.

Introduction

The extent to which technology has affected, and continues to affect, our lives is immeasurable. Today, the use of apps, cloud technology, and the Internet of Things are e gina strazzabosco ny veryday concepts. The evolution of apps in particular has changed the way many people travel, eat, and get things done around the house. And daily, companies emerge by way of user-friendly, cost-effective, and truly innovative apps.

Many of these businesses are rooted in the sharing economy, also known as the "peer" or "gig" economy. The first companies of this nature that come to mind for most people are Uber and Airbnb. There are nuances between these businesses: some are structured around owners (of, say, apartments or castles or bicycles) who rent out what they own when not in use. Airbnb is the ideal example of this. Alternatively, some, like Uber and TaskRabbit, are structured on a business model where individuals use an app to find someone to perform a service for them (like picking them up at a bar or dropping off their dry cleaning).

Technological advances are not the only forces driving the sharing economy. For many individuals, millennials in particular, a need for access is key as well—particularly a need for access to items or services where ownership is simply cost prohibitive. According to "How Millennials Are Defining the Sharing Economy" (*Entrepreneur,* June 9, 2016), the uncertain economy in which millennials have grown up has contributed to an inborn-like need for frugality, and the social connection that's new and awkward for some is just part of how most millennials operate and communicate anyway.

The blog *The People Who Share* (thepeoplewhoshare.com) offers a clear definition that also provides a strong foundation for this book's discussion and coverage of the sharing economy: "The Sharing Economy is a socio-economic ecosystem built around the sharing of human, physical and intellectual resources. It includes the shared creation, production, distribution, trade and consumption of goods and services by different people and organisations." To be clear, the word "sharing" is not to imply that there is no cost involved. There is, in most cases, an exchange of fees for goods or services rendered.

In December 2015, the Pew Research Center performed its first research study on this topic, during which 4,787 Americans were surveyed. Entitled "Shared, Collaborative and On Demand: The New Digital Economy," the survey revealed that while 73% of participants were not familiar with the term "sharing economy," 72% had indeed "used some type of shared or on-demand service." The research revealed a clear disparity in awareness based on age, with a drop off in awareness for participants over forty-five years of age. Other factors, including household income and education, also come into play, but these are ever-evolving pieces of a puzzle that is being put together and taken apart—and then put back together—on a daily basis, around the world.

In a 2016 survey conducted by *The People Who Share*'s team, in partnership with identity-verification company Veridu, participants in the United States and the United Kingdom revealed, unsurprisingly, that an overwhelming majority of respondents put personal safety and saving money at the top of their priority list. People see participation in the sharing economy as a way to cut back on expenses, but also are wary of risks to their own personal safety and that of their loved ones.

Opposing Viewpoints: Uber, Lyft, Airbnb, and the Sharing Economy examines the structure and makeup of the sharing economy, and the issues facing consumers, government, conventional businesses, and new businesses. Chapters include "Is the 'Sharing Economy' Really About Sharing?," "How Do the Sharing Economy and Conventional Businesses Affect One Another?," "Who Benefits from the Sharing Economy?," and "Is the Sharing Economy Here to Stay?" The moving-target nature of this newer element within our already complicated economy makes it a tough-yet-interesting area to track, and one that's definitely worth our attention.

CHAPTER 1

Is the "Sharing Economy" Really About Sharing?

Chapter Preface

C hanges in the ways in which we communicate, shop, and think about our needs all contributed to the start of the sharing economy, several years ago. Sometimes called the gig economy or the peer-to-peer economy, among other names, the businesses that fall into this category have opened the door for an infinite number of challenges and questions. From ethics, to privacy concerns, to the rights of entrepreneurs versus the rights of conventional, long-standing businesses, the sharing economy continues to hold the spotlight of many a heated debate.

The legality of the business models explored in this chapter will be discussed, as will the ways in which big businesses—and sometimes small ones as well—evolve in their response to the peer-to-peer economy.

This chapter explores the structure of the sharing economy using the examples of peer-to-peer businesses such as Uber, Lyft, Airbnb, Task Rabbit, and others. It will examine whether this structure really constitutes "sharing" and how collaboration fits in.

The importance of regulations is another widely covered aspect of the sharing economy and one that will be covered in this chapter. By way of the articles that follow, you'll have the opportunity to consider whether the sharing economy has reduced the democratic nature of this sector. Elements to consider on this topic include what laws are currently in place and whether they are obsolete, what gaps need to be filled in terms of regulations, and what abuses of the system are happening—or at risk of happening—and how can they be mitigated or, better yet, prevented.

This chapter also examines the building blocks of the sharing economy, the terminology used to describe the sharing economy, and the ramifications (or lack thereof) on record for companies that do not comply with shifts in laws and newly implemented regulations. The authors of the featured viewpoints span a wide range of opinions, and some even acknowledge their own changes of heart in recent months and years.

| "A Sharing Economy enables different forms of value exchange and is a hybrid economy."

A Sharing Economy Creates a Sharing Society

Benita Matofska

In the following viewpoint, Benita Matofska offers a clear and firm definition of the term "sharing economy," which she categorizes as a sustainable economic ecosystem. She provides a list of the ten building blocks that make up the sharing economy, from her perspective. Benita Matofska is the founder of The People Who Share *and the author of the annual report* What We Know About the Global Sharing Economy. *She is an RSA Fellow, an Innovator in the Finance Innovation Lab, and a member of the Astia women's network.*

As you read, consider the following questions:

1. According to the author, how many building blocks make up the sustainable economic ecosystem of the sharing economy?
2. According to the author, how does a sharing economy empower citizens?
3. According to the viewpoint, what are the three types of resources around which the sharing economy is built?

"What Is the Sharing Economy?" by Benita Matofska, *The People Who Share*, September 1, 2016. Reprinted by permission.

The Sharing Economy is a socio-economic ecosystem built around the sharing of human, physical and intellectual resources.

It includes the shared creation, production, distribution, trade and consumption of goods and services by different people and organisations.

Whilst the Sharing Economy is currently in its infancy, known most notably as a series of services and start-ups which enable P2P exchanges through technology, this is only the beginning: in its entirety and potential it is a new and alternative socio-economic system which embeds sharing and collaboration at its heart – across all aspects of social and economic life.

The 'Sharing' in the Sharing Economy refers to the use and access of shared physical or human resources or assets, rather than the fact that there is no monetary exchange. A Sharing Economy enables different forms of value exchange and is a hybrid economy. It encompasses the following aspects: swapping, exchanging, collective purchasing, collaborative consumption, shared ownership, shared value, co-operatives, co-creation, recycling, upcycling, re-distribution, trading used goods, renting, borrowing, lending, subscription based models, peer-to-peer, collaborative economy, circular economy, on-demand economy, gig economy, crowd economy, pay-as-you-use economy, wikinomics, peer-to-peer lending, micro financing, micro-entrepreneurship, social media, the Mesh, social enterprise, futurology, crowdfunding, crowdsourcing, cradle-to-cradle, open source, open data, user generated content (UGC) and public services.

A Sharing Economy is a sustainable economic ecosystem comprised of the following 10 building blocks:

1. People

People are at the heart of a Sharing Economy; it is a People's Economy, meaning that people are active citizens and participants of their communities and the wider society. The participants of a Sharing Economy are individuals, communities, companies, organisations and associations, all of whom are deeply embedded in a highly efficient sharing system, to which all contribute and benefit from. Human rights are respected and safeguarded. People are also suppliers of goods and services; they are creators, collaborators, producers, co-producers, distributors and re-distributors. In a Sharing Economy, people create, collaborate, produce and distribute peer-to-peer, person-to-person (P2P). Micro-entrepreneurship is celebrated, where people can enter into binding contracts with one another and trade peer-to-peer (P2P). Within business, people – both co-owners, employees and customers – are highly valued, with their opinions and ideas respected and integrated into the business at all levels of the supply chain, organisation and development. I call the people who are driving the Sharing Economy, Generation Share.

2. Production

In a Sharing Economy, people, organisations and communities as active participants produce or co-produce goods and services collaboratively or collectively or co-operatively. Production is open and accessible to those who wish to produce. Internet technologies and networks enable the development of products and services in a collective manner, transcending geographical boundaries. Local production with positive (or minimal) environmental impacts is celebrated. 3D printing offers a more local production of goods, shortening supply chains and increasing efficiency and access. Social responsibility is strong and public services (including social support) are co-produced – developed and provided – by a wide range of actors acting across social levels; families and friends, local communities, charities, social enterprises, business and government.

3. Value & Systems of Exchange

A Sharing Economy is a hybrid economy where there are a variety of forms of exchange, incentives and value creation. Value is seen not purely as financial value, but wider economic, environmental and social value are equally important, accounted for and sought after. The system embraces alternative currencies, local currencies, timebanks, social investment and social capital. The Sharing Economy is based on both material and non-material or social rewards and encourages the most efficient use of resources. This hybrid incentive system enables and motivates people to engage in productive activities. In a Sharing Economy, waste has value, it is viewed as resource in the wrong place. A Sharing Economy enables 'waste' to be reallocated where it is needed and valued.

4. Distribution

In a Sharing Economy, resources are distributed and redistributed via a system that is both efficient and equitable on a local, regional, national and global scale. Shared ownership models such as cooperatives, collective purchasing and collaborative consumption are features of a Sharing Economy, promoting a fair distribution of assets that benefits society as a whole. Participatory democratic systems enable the development of structures and legislation that promote and safeguard an equitable and efficient distribution of resources at all scales of society.

Idle resources are re-allocated or traded with those who want or need them to create an efficient, equitable, closed loop or circular system. Recycling, upcycling and sharing the lifecycle of the product are features common to a Sharing Economy. 'Waste' is viewed as 'resource in the wrong place' and the system uses technology to re-distribute or trade unused or 'sleeping' assets, generating value for people, communities and companies. Access is promoted and preferred over ownership and seen as distributed or shared ownership. Being a member of a car club, for example, and paying for what you use, is seen as preferable and smarter than bearing the cost, burden, resource wastage and idling capacity of ownership.

5. Planet

A Sharing Economy puts both people and planet at the heart of the economic system. Value creation, production and distribution operate in synergy or harmony with the available natural resources, not at the expense of the planet, promoting the flourishing of human life within environmental limits. Environmental responsibility, including the burdens of environmental damage, are shared; among people, organisations, and national governments.

Goods and services within a Sharing Economy are designed for sustainability rather than obsolescence, promoting not only the re-use of resources, but also models that have a positive impact on the planet. For example, rather than simply reducing negative impact through carbon reduction, a Sharing Economy creates goods and services that positively enhance the natural environment, such as cradle-to-cradle (C2C) or circular economy models. An example would be a pair of trainers made from recycled materials that have seeds implanted in their biodegradable soles; as the trainers degrade, plants grow.

6. Power

A Sharing Economy both empowers its citizens economically and socially and enables the economic and social redistribution of power. Both facets hinge on an open, shared, distributed, democratic decision-making process and governance systems, at the local, national and global level. This robust ecosystem facilitates this opening and sharing of opportunities and access to power. Power is shared or distributed and the infrastructure enables citizens to access power and decision-making. Systems that enable and promote fair pay, reduce inequality and poverty such as Fairtrade are supported and preferred. It supports people to become active citizens, deeply engaged in their communities and in the development of the environments they live and work in.

7. Shared Law

In a Sharing Economy, the mechanism for law making is democratic, public and accessible. Rules, policies, laws and standards are created via a democratic system that enables and encourages mass participation at all levels. Laws and policies support, enable and incentivise sharing practices among citizens and within business, such as car sharing, peer-to-peer trading and a variety of forms of resource sharing. Laws, policies, structures and infrastructure create a system of trust with insurances, assurances, social ratings and reputation capital at the forefront.

8. Communications

In a Sharing Economy, information and knowledge is shared, open and accessible. Good, open communications are central to the flow, efficiency and sustainability of this economic system. A fundamental tenant of the Sharing Economy is that communications are distributed, knowledge and intelligence are widely accessible, easily obtained and can be used by different individuals, communities or organisations and used in a variety of different ways for a myriad of purposes. Technology and social networks enable the flow of communications and support the sharing of information. This system promotes easily accessible education of a high level, through a wide range of diverse services (both public and private), enabling everyone to access the information, skills and tools they need to succeed. Promoting the message 'Share More' is at the heart of Sharing Economy communications.

9. Culture

The Sharing Economy promotes a WE based culture where the wider community and the greater good are considered. Health, happiness, trust and sustainability are notable characteristics. Sharing is seen as a positive attribute, people who share are celebrated, encouraged and enabled. A shareable lifestyle is championed and preferred. A sharing culture is embedded across sectors, geographies, economic backgrounds, genders, religions and ethnicities. Diversity is celebrated, collaborations between different groups applauded and incentivised. Sharing and collaboration are seen as the vital lifeline connecting groups at all levels; from the individual local level, to that of neighbouring communities, to that of nation states and supranational bodies.

The sharing of resources is part of the fabric and eco-system of a sharing society; externalities are always considered and integrated. Business culture is based around the most efficient use of resources and a collaborative business culture. Conscious business, social business, sustainable business, ethical business, social enterprise, business as a force for good are also features of a Sharing Economy. The predominant business models of a Sharing Economy are: access based models, services, subscription, rental, collaborative and peer-to-peer models. Disruptive innovation, sharepreneurship, creative entrepreneurship, intrapreneuship and micro-entrepreneurship are common features of a Sharing Economy.

10. Future

A Sharing Economy is a robust, sustainable economic system that is built around a long term vision, always considering the impact and consequences of present day actions on the future. By considering long-term implications, futurology and being able to see the 'big picture', a Sharing Economy presents a stable and sustainable economic system. Systems thinking, and the need for a systemic approach to change is fundamental to the success of the Sharing Economy.

> *"As the economic power of these technology-driven firms grows, there continue to be regulatory and policy skirmishes on every possible front, across cities and towns spanning the United States, Europe and beyond."*

The Gig Economy Is Still Unchartered Territory

Joanna Penn and John Wihbey

In the following viewpoint, Joanna Penn and John Wihbey point out the challenges created by start-up businesses that are part of the so-called "gig" economy. They cover several ways in which conventional businesses and governments have pushed back on this newer option for consumers, primarily in the form of lawsuits and proposed or new legislation. They also share examples of how long-standing businesses are getting into the game themselves. Joanna Penn is the author of several books about writing and the creative process, and is the founder of the blog thecreativepenn.com. John Wihbey is an Assistant Professor of journalism and new media at Northeastern University. His writing credits include the Boston Globe, Pacific Standard, Nieman Journalism Lab, *and* Yale Climate Connections.

As you read, consider the following questions:

1. According to the authors, is the workforce in the United States expected to increase, decrease, or stay the same over the next several years?
2. According to this viewpoint, what are some of the potential risks to workers within the sharing economy as it grows?
3. According to this viewpoint, what European city, in 2014, became the first to implement so-called "Airbnb friendly" legislation?

The leading businesses that are advancing the concept of the "sharing economy" are in many respects no longer insurgents and newcomers. The size and scale of Uber, Airbnb and several other firms now rival, or even surpass, those of some of the world's largest businesses in transportation, hospitality and other sectors. As the economic power of these technology-driven firms grows, there continue to be regulatory and policy skirmishes on every possible front, across cities and towns spanning the United States, Europe and beyond.

While many municipalities and regions have accepted change as inevitable and have been eager to facilitate new efficiencies for consumers — Uber in particular has made a lot of regulatory headway since 2015 — there have been cases, such as in Austin, Tex. in May 2016, where policies have been in effect reversed to block these new forms of commerce. These fights are looking more and more like political campaigns. In any case, a 2015 report from the National League of Cities reviews regulatory policies and patterns across a variety of dimensions, from safety to innovation; a 2016 report from the European Parliament weighs the costs and benefits of non-participation in the sharing economy.

The Economics and Statistics Administration of the U.S. Commerce Department issued a report in June 2016 that attempts to define and map out the contours of this emerging business sector, labeling its participants "digital matching firms." That report defines this sector through the four following characteristics:

- They use information technology (IT systems), typically available via web-based platforms, such as mobile "apps" on Internet-enabled devices, to facilitate peer-to-peer transactions.
- They rely on user-based rating systems for quality control, ensuring a level of trust between consumers and service providers who have not previously met.
- They offer the workers who provide services via digital matching platforms flexibility in deciding their typical working hours.
- To the extent that tools and assets are necessary to provide a service, digital matching firms rely on the workers using their own.

The implications of the sharing economy — part of what has also been termed the "gig economy" — have of course been hotly debated in the news media, and the research world has been steadily weighing in with deeper analysis. One central area of argument relates to whether the sharing economy is simply bringing more wage-earning opportunities to more people, or whether its net effect is the displacement of traditionally secure jobs and the creation of a land of part-time, low-paid work. It's a debate that continues to develop and play out, forcing reporters to weigh competing claims that vary in tone from boosterism to warnings of the new economy's "dark side."

While the conclusions about the overall effects of this sector are anything but clear, even as more data pour in, it is worth digging into the available literature and knowing the centers of research debate and lines of argument.

A January 2015 paper co-authored by Princeton's Alan Krueger — the former Chairman of President Barack Obama's Council of Economic Advisers — based on Uber's internal data finds clear benefits for "driver-partners" and notes the new financial opportunities created for tens of thousands of workers. Those conclusions have been critiqued by, for example, the liberal-leaning Center for Economic and Policy Research. In any case, the Krueger paper also argues that "the availability of modern technology, like the Uber app, provides many advantages and lower prices for consumers compared with the traditional taxi cab dispatch system, and this has boosted demand for ride services, which, in turn, has increased total demand for workers with the requisite skills to work as for-hire drivers, potentially raising earnings for all workers with such skills."

There is the distinct danger, on both sides, of overstating the case and the size of effects. A 2014 paper by Annette Bernhardt of University of California, Berkeley, signals a cautionary note about any claims of radical recent change being wrought across the U.S. economy:

[We] all share a strong intuition that the nature of work has fundamentally changed, contributing to the deterioration of labor standards. Yet at least with aggregate national data, it has been hard to find evidence of a strong, unambiguous shift toward nonstandard or contingent forms of work – especially in contrast to the dramatic increase in wage inequality. This is not to say that there have been no changes in the workplace. But as this paper has emphasized, for enforcement agencies and policymakers, it may be more fruitful to focus on specific industries and regions in assessing when and where pernicious forms of nonstandard work have grown, and which groups of workers have been most impacted.

It is also true that the rise of independent workers, and associated job insecurity, long predates the recent rise of the sharing economy, although their percentage of all U.S. workers is expected to grow from about one-third currently to 40% by 2020, according to some estimates.

A 2015 report from the Center for American Progress notes the heated debate in Britain over "zero hours contracts" and charges that highly insecure and contingent employment leads to the exploitation of workers. The report — co-authored by Harvard's

REGULATION'S INEVITABILITY

Regulation is often the most significant barrier to future growth for sharing economy firms. This is particularly unfortunate since the incentives of city governments and sharing economy firms are often aligned. Given the benefits these types of firms bring to cities and firms' vested interest in the very consumer protections that city governments are seeking to ensure, one would expect a less rocky start for these new entrants.

The relationship between sharing economy firms and regulators will likely remain uneasy for the foreseeable future. But companies in this space can benefit from being more cooperative with regulators. As a manager in a sharing economy firm, you can increase the growth of your firm, reduce unnecessary delays, avoid conflict with regulators and expand access for consumers [...].

"How Uber and the Sharing Economy Can Win Over Regulators," by Sarah Cannon and Lawrence H. Summers, *Harvard Business Review,* October 13, 2014.

Lawrence Summers, a top official in both the Clinton and Obama administrations, and Ed Balls, a British Labour Party MP — notes that "technology has allowed a sharing economy to develop in the United States; many of these jobs offer flexibility to workers, many of whom are working a second job and using it to build income or are parents looking for flexible work schedules. At the same time, when these jobs are the only source of income for workers and they provide no benefits, that leaves workers or the state to pay these costs."

Meanwhile, scholars such as Juliet Schor of Boston College have been examining how workers might regain bargaining power despite an increasingly app-based, decentralized system of distributed labor. "While the for-profit companies may be 'acting badly,'" she writes in an October 2014 essay, "these new technologies of peer-to-peer economic activity are potentially powerful tools for building a social movement centered on genuine practices of sharing and cooperation in the production and consumption of goods and services. But achieving that potential will require democratizing the ownership and governance of the platforms."

Fights over rules and regulations

In October 2014 the New York State Attorney General released a report into Airbnb's operations that concluded that 72% of the site's rentals violated state zoning regulations or other laws. The company's business model is built around allowing people to rent out rooms or entire apartments on a short-term basis, and the report is the latest in a series of ongoing battles Airbnb is engaged in with regulators across the world.

Berlin has banned regular short-term rentals in the most popular parts of the city without prior permission from the authorities. Paris passed a law in February 2014 to allow city inspectors to check rental homes whose owners are suspected of renting them out to visitors illegally. Airbnb has countered with its own reports on the benefits of short-term stays on local housing markets, arguing that the company's service benefits local economies.

Also known as collaborative consumption or peer-to-peer (P2P), the sharing economy challenges traditional notions of private ownership and is instead based on the shared production or consumption of goods and services. Its origins were in not-for-profit initiatives such as Wikipedia (2001) and Couchsurfing and Freecycle (both 2003). Advances in information technology enabled the creation of large-scale bike-share systems (the first was in Lyon, France, in 2005), and these have subsequently expanded to the United States and around the world.

Social media and mobile technology have enabled the latest expansion of the sharing economy and turned it into a big business: Airbnb allows individuals to share their homes, while Lyft and Uber transform private cars into common resources. All these are for-profit services, but they take only a fraction of the fees levied, passing the rest on to the owners: In 2013 it was estimated that revenues passing through the sharing economy into people's wallets exceeded $3.5 billion, up 25% from the previous year. Airbnb has exceeded 10 million guest-stays since its launch and now has more than half a million properties listed. Meanwhile Uber has said that it is doubling its revenue every six months.

As a 2014 article in *Harvard Business Review* noted, the interests of sharing-economy firms and city governments are often aligned, but failing to engage early on with potential regulators can raise the suspicion that companies are trying to exploit loopholes rather than develop a legitimate business model. For example, courts in Frankfurt recently upheld a national ban on Uber, and the service has been banned in several Canadian cities as well. At the heart of many of these debates is whether Uber is, as it claims, operating as a pure technology company, providing a match-making service to willing participants, or whether it is operating in effect as an unlicensed taxi service, which was the conclusion of Calgary's city council. Moreover, a Massachusetts class-action lawsuit asserts that Uber exploits its drivers, misclassifying them as independent contractors to avoid paying them as employees with the same benefits.

Examples from elsewhere in the world shows such fractious relationships with regulators need not be the norm. In February 2014, Amsterdam became the first city to pass so-called "Airbnb friendly" legislation. A law allowing short-term rentals by permanent San Francisco residents was finalized in October 2014, but requires them to collect city hotel taxes and imposes other restrictions. In London, 1970s regulations limiting short-term stays were scrapped, making it easier for Airbnb and others to operate in the city. The British government has even launched an initiative to make the U.K. the "global centre for [the] sharing economy." Similarly, while some traditional operators have fought sharing start-ups, others have chosen to get in on the game themselves: In 2013 Avis paid half a billion dollars for the car-sharing service Zipcar, and Hertz has started a similar service.

> "As allegedly 'innovative' firms increasingly influence our economy and culture, they must be held accountable for the power they exercise."

The Problem with Corporate Nullification

Frank Pasquale and Siva Vaidhyanathan

In the following viewpoint, Frank Pasquale and Siva Vaidhyanathan argue that the efforts behind corporate nullification ultimately have negative effects on society and can increase the likelihood of conflict. They liken the practice to efforts of some Southern governors in the 1950s and 1960s, to find ways "around" following then-recently passed civil rights laws. Pasquale is the author of Black Box Society: The Secret Algorithms that Control Money and Information *(Harvard University Press, 2015). Vaidhyanathan is the author of* The Googlization of Everything—and Why We Should Worry *(University of California Press, 2011).*

As you read, consider the following questions:

1. According to the authors, what historical figures did proponents of Uber and Airbnb compare the companies to?
2. According to this viewpoint, what city's mayor unsuccessfully pushed back against the onslaught of Uber drivers?
3. According to the authors, what Google project put the burden of removing their information for privacy protection on the general population?

In February, Airbnb chief executive Brian Chesky compared his firm's defiance of local housing ordinances with that of Gandhi's passive resistance to British rule. Meanwhile, a tweeter compared Uber to Rosa Parks, defying unjust laws. Chesky quickly backed down after widespread mockery. Companies acting out of self-interest comparing themselves with the noble heroes of civil rights movements is as absurd as it is insulting.

But there is a better analogy from the US civil rights era for law-flouting firms of the on-demand economy. It's just not the one corporate leaders claim. They are engaged in what we call "corporate nullification", following in the footsteps of Southern governors and legislatures in the United States who declared themselves free to "nullify" federal law on the basis of strained and opportunistic constitutional interpretation.

Nullification is a willful flouting of regulation, based on some nebulous idea of a higher good only scofflaws can deliver. It can be an invitation to escalate a conflict, of course, as Arkansas governor Orville Faubus did in 1957 when he refused to desegregate public schools and president Eisenhower sent federal troops to enforce the law. But when companies such as Uber, Airbnb, and Google engage in a nullification effort, it's a libertarian-inspired attempt to establish their services as popular well before regulators can get around to confronting them. Then, when officials push back, they can appeal to their consumer-following to push regulators to surrender.

This happened just last week in New York City, when mayor Bill de Blasio moved to limit the number of Uber cars choking city streets during the heaviest hours of congestion. Uber pushed out advertisements voiced by celebrities including model Kate Upton and urged its wealthy users to write to city hall in protest. Mayor de Blasio stood down. Consistently, these nullifying companies claim they are striking a blow against regulations they consider "out-of-date" or "anti-innovation." Their major innovation, however, is strategic and manipulative, and it's meant to undermine local needs and effective governance.

Between 2005 and 2010 Google shot photos of much of the world – and many of its people – without permission for its Street View project, often pushing the limits of privacy laws along the way. In addition, Google hoovered up data from Wi-Fi networks that its cars passed through. To this day, Google has not explained why it captured all that private data. It worked. Despite some incidents in which Google had to reshoot the street scenes most regulators backed down because the public had grown used to the service or Google appeased them somehow.

Google's strategy was to flip the defaults: Anyone who took issue with a shot on Street View was welcome to apply to have it removed. So it became our burden, not Google's, to protect privacy. Google engaged in the same strategy of shoot (digital images) first and answer questions later when scanning copyrighted books. Some people got mad over these bold moves. Some people sued. Google worked through the conflicts later – sometimes by winning in court (as in the case of book scanning) and sometimes by losing rulings in Australia, South Korea, and Japan, and Greece, where Street View was ruled illegal in 2009.

The analogy is most obvious in the case of an American civil rights law itself. Uber has ignored advocates for the blind, and other disabled persons, when they claim Uber's drivers discriminate against them. In response to a lawsuit by the National Federation of the Blind, Uber bluntly asserts that it's merely a communication platform, not the type of employer meant to be covered by the Americans with Disabilities Act. Some judges and regulators accept that reasoning; others reject it. But the larger lesson is clear: Uber's aggressive efforts to avoid or evade disability laws are nothing less than a form of corporate nullification, as menacing to the rule of law as defiance of civil rights laws in the days after courts ruled against racial segregation in the US.

In addition, Uber has confronted admittedly stifling restrictions on taxi driver licenses in France by launching a service called UberPop. Several authorities in Europe have ruled UberPop illegal, but Uber kept it operating anyway as it appealed. Now France has charged Uber's general director for France, Thibaud Simphal, and the company's director for Western Europe, Pierre-Dimitri Gore-Coty with enabling taxi-driving by non-professional drivers and "deceptive commercial practices."

One could make a strong argument that France would benefit from more taxi drivers and more competition. But that's for the people of France to decide through their elected representatives. The spirit of Silicon Valley should not dictate policy for the rest of the world. New York, Paris, London, Cairo, and New Delhi all have different values and traffic issues. Local needs should be respected.

Consider what it would mean for such a universalising approach to prevail. The business model of Uber would become that of law-flouting bosses generally. Reincorporate as a "platform," intermediate customer requests and work demands with an app, and voila!, far fewer laws to comply with. Worse, this rebel attitude signals to the larger culture that laws and regulations are quaint and archaic, and therefore hindrances to progress. That could undermine faith in republican government itself.

In the 1950s and 60s, Southern governors thought they'd found a similar tactic to avoid the civil rights laws that they most despised. Though the strategy failed, the idea still animates reactionaries. Former Arkansas governor Mike Huckabee, now running for president, has even suggested that the US supreme court's recent gay marriage decision should effectively be nullified by sovereign states.

Of course, a republic can't run without authorities who follow the rule of law. Civil disobedience by citizens can be an important challenge to corrupt or immoral politicians, but when corporate leaders themselves start breaking the law in their own narrow interests, societal order breaks down. Polishing their left-libertarian veneer, the on-demand economy firms now flouting basic employment and anti-discrimination laws would like us to believe that they follow in the footsteps of Gandhi's passive resistance, rather than segregationists' massive resistance. But their wealthy, powerful, nearly-all-white-and-male cast of chief executives come far closer to embodying, rather than fighting, "the man".

As Silicon Valley guru Peter Thiel has demonstrated, the goal of tech firms is not to compete – it is to so monopolise a sector that they basically become synonymous with it. Uber's and Airbnb's self-reinforcing conquests of markets attract more venture capital (VC) investment, which in turn enables more conquests, which in turn attracts more VC money. As that concentration of economic power continues apace, it's more vital than ever to dispute Silicon Valley oligarchs' self-aggrandising assertions that they follow in the footsteps of civil rights heroes.

As allegedly "innovative" firms increasingly influence our economy and culture, they must be held accountable for the power they exercise. Otherwise, corporate nullification will further entrench a two-tier system of justice, where individuals and small firms abide by one set of laws, and mega-firms create their own regime of privilege for themselves and power over others.

> "*Understanding the social and economic motivations for and implications of participating in the sharing economy is important to its regulation.*"

We Must Understand the Sharing Economy Before Trying to Regulate It

Kristofer Erickson

In the following viewpoint, Kristofer Erickson explores the various ways in which consumers and businesses can—and do—define "sharing." He examines the use of the word from a social standpoint as well as from an economic standpoint. Erickson also points out regulatory challenges as they relate to aspects of the sharing economy, including working conditions, trust, risk, liability, and individual agency. Erickson is an editor at Internet Policy Review, *a lecturer at the University of Glasgow, and cofounder of* Copyright User *and* Copyright Evidence Wiki.

As you read, consider the following questions:

1. How do previously anonymous participants now communicate, according to the author?
2. According to this viewpoint, what risks do platform operators face when it comes to peer-to-peer networks?
3. What are some of the concerns the author points out about reliance on user ratings?

Abstract

In this introductory essay, we explore definitions of the 'sharing economy,' a concept indicating both social (relational, communitarian) and economic (allocative, profit-seeking) aspects which appear to be in tension. We suggest combining the social and economic logics of the sharing economy to focus on the central features of network enabled, aggregated membership in a pool of offers and demands (for goods, services, creative expressions). This definition of the sharing economy distinguishes it from other related peer-to-peer and collaborative forms of production. Understanding the social and economic motivations for and implications of participating in the sharing economy is important to its regulation. Each of the papers in this special issue contributes to knowledge by linking the social and economic aspects of sharing economy practices to regulatory norms and mechanisms. We conclude this essay by suggesting future research to further clarify and render intelligible the sharing economy, not as a contradiction in terms but as an empirically observable realm of socio-economic activity.

Introduction: What "Sharing?"

The sharing economy is on the rise. In 2015 gross revenue from sharing economy companies across the EU doubled from 2014 and totaled 28 billion EUR (EU, 2016) and it is estimated to be worth 335 billion USD globally by 2025 (PriceWaterhouseCoopers, 2015). A third of Europeans have used the services of a sharing platform (EU, 2016), rising to 72% of North Americans (Pew

Research Center, 2016). Today, there is little dispute that the sharing economy impacts lives and livelihoods and that technologies underpinning it both structure behaviour and facilitate emerging and expanding business. Yet, as ongoing and numerous legal actions and injunctions against companies like Uber and Airbnb across the world demonstrate[1], opinion differs on the extent to which the sharing economy should be regulated, resisted or embraced. Similarly, there is little research into how the technological affordances and infrastructures that underpin the sharing economy structure and shape human interactions and transactions, and, crucially, what this means in a wider cultural or socio-economic context. This special issue seeks to address this.

One obstacle to a deeper understanding of the 'sharing economy' has been ambiguity about its definition. Sharing, which evokes familiar exchanges and intimate relationships, seems to be at odds with economic activity driven by anonymous transactions and rational, rather than altruistic behaviour (Belk, 2010; Schor et al, 2015). Political debates about the status of sharing economy services highlight tensions in the social and economic dimensions of these new services. The way that society and policymakers define the sharing economy will influence how we choose to regulate its activities. The purpose of this introduction to the special issue is firstly, to provide a definition of the sharing economy and secondly, to discuss how empirical approaches, such as the contributions to this collection, can help inform policy concerns.

In brief, we advance a definition of the sharing economy which incorporates both its social and economic relationality. For us, the present 'sharing economy' is defined by the *aggregation* of individual offers (of goods, labour, creative expression) into a common pool. The practice of sharing in our proposed definition is not dependent on shared ownership or access to products or services, since sharing economy goods may be excluded from those who do not pay. Rather it is the shared, collective status of users who offer something of their own to the aggregated pool which constitutes mutuality (in however weak a form).

Networked, mobile technologies make possible communication between previously anonymous participants, and can foster a range of reciprocal and non-reciprocal interaction. However, unlike gift economies where reciprocity aids in strengthening group ties, or commons-based peer production where ownership of collaboration is shared, commercial sharing economy platforms are not held together by reciprocity or shared ownership of goods. Consumers of these services may come and go: they may be inspired after a successful transaction to join the service with an offer of their own, or they may not.

Sharing economy goods are typically excludable and rivalrous (for example a bicycle sharing app which permits paying customers exclusive use of a peer's bicycle for an appointed period of time). Consequently, the goods exchanged in the sharing economy do not themselves constitute a shared commons. This highlights one of the faultlines in debates about the status of sharing in the sharing economy. In traditional societies as well as certain forms of commons-based peer production, the beneficiaries of sharing are also contributors themselves (that is, sharing practices are interwoven with social and political capital and group membership). Now, anonymous, decentralised, peer-to-peer matchmaking replaces pre-existing social ties, leading to new political and economic subjectivities (Schor et al., 2015; Erickson, 2015). However, as we discuss below, social and personal motivations for taking part in aggregated sharing economy markets remain key to their growth as well as the policies designed to regulate them. We thus cannot ignore the social and relational features present alongside economic incentives in the commercial sharing economy.

Social Features, from Peer-to-Peer to Collaborative Consumption

'Sharing' has been a social and transactional practice long before it was coupled with 'economy', of course, and is neither new to the internet nor society at large. Some have argued that the practice of sharing is hardwired into humans as social beings and is a necessity for survival (Price (1975) as cited in Belk, 2009, p. 715 and Nicholson, 1998). Sharing is integral to the socialisation process that takes place from childhood in most communities. The right to decide what is being shared and amongst whom varies culturally, and reflects the norms and hegemonies within a given society (Belk, 2009; Tomasello et al., 2005, pp. 683-4). In democracies with social-democratic leanings this is often imbued with social responsibility; for example, infants in the English-speaking world learn that 'sharing is caring'.

From early in its inception, the web was envisaged as an open space for all to share information (The World Wide Web Foundation, 2016). In line with this, a large body of academic work explored both reciprocal and non-reciprocal modes of sharing, motivated by a range of rewards, such as for example explored by Barbrook (1998), Benkler (2004; 2006), Boyle (2003: 45) and Lessig (2008). Analyses of online sharing practices such as these focused on the peer-to-peer, non-hierarchical features of networks of commons-based production. Digital networks appeared to flatten hierarchies in numerous ways, such as by cutting out intermediaries and gatekeepers that were seen as commercially-driven profiteers or restrictive of creative freedom.

It is precisely these prerequisites for effective peer-to-peer (p2p) sharing networks and communities, that have precipitated the 'sharing economy'. With Web 2.0, the growth of the 'sharing economy' has been propelled by at least two factors: networked p2p communication enabled by digital innovation on the one hand, and on the other technological advances in online banking enabling consumers to make secure transactions and micropayments (features that Jenkins (2004: 39) identified as facilitating 'convergence'). The convergence between the affordances of social media platforms and the economic propositions based on sharing of resources and secure transactional technologies, combined with circumnavigation of traditional intermediaries, form the foundation of what constitutes the sharing economy today and the new commercial transnational players and gatekeepers therein (Van Dijck, 2013).

This paradox lies at the core of the debates that surround sharing economy practices today. On the one hand the discourse – and for some, reality – of sharing resonates with community, reciprocity, equality, flexibility and freedom from interference by intermediaries. This is supported by the fact that non-reciprocal sharing platforms and economies evidently work effectively and inspire their communities. For example, crowd-sharing practices flourish on Freecycle where recycled and reused goods are exchanged in kind (Phipps, 2015). Helpful contributors to the Mumsnet community advise on products and activities for young families. Crowdfunding platforms like Kickstarter and Indiegogo do the work of arts funders and enterprise offices (Sørensen, 2013). It is of course important to note that both crowdwork and the reasons for engaging in such ventures predate the internet. For example, patronage of the arts goes back to at least antiquity and operated on a near industrial scale in Renaissance Italy. The first Oxford English dictionary was co-created by a group of contributors in 1858 and long preceded Wikipedia. Today and then, these practices and participation in sharing and collaborative ventures are motivated by a variety of factors. For example, patronage; the wish to 'do good'; the feeling of belonging to a community; and the social status or capital accrued by the act of sharing (Benkler, 2012, 2014; Belk, 2009; Mollick, 2014). In the case of new sharing economy platforms - even when sharing is mediated by a transaction and occurs between strangers - many of the same intrinsic motivations appear to remain (Phipps, 2015).

Although on many sharing economy platforms social ties between participants are weak or non-existent, a discourse of sociality continues to be adopted by commercial networks and players in the market (Lury, 2015). Notions of collaboration, freedom and flexibility are offered in response to challenges which include poor working conditions, liability and lack of regulation (Newsnight, BBC2, 2016). These practical and discursive dissonances around sharing economies complicate the analysis of their dynamics.

Economic Features: Private Goods, Club Goods or Common Resources?

Economic definitions of the sharing economy focus on the efficient allocation of resources through mutual agreement by networked participants to grant access to goods or services they own. Economic 'gains from sharing' are realised as previously underutilised private goods are made available to more consumers (Fremstad, 2016). Sharing economy exchanges may be reciprocal or non-reciprocal, however an important distinguishing feature is that the aggregated, p2p organisation of sharing platforms does not require users to return an equivalent product or service to the pool. One could choose to always remain a consumer, or a provider, of goods. Highlighting the consumptive, coordinated market character of the practice, the sharing economy has also been closely identified with 'collaborative consumption' (Belk, 2014) or 'access economy' (Eckhardt & Bardhi, 2015).

At its core, the sharing economy consists of an agreement between participants to contribute an owned resource (labour, goods, creative expression) to a common pool from which others may draw, with or without a commercial transaction. The benefits to the contributing participant are potentially (i) a share in the reduction of transaction costs[2] achieved by collectively aggregating the exchange, (ii) access to a larger market attracted by the size of the aggregated offer. The customer in a sharing economy transaction likewise benefits from reduced costs (i), while also being able to browse a larger collection of offers (ii).

Operators of sharing economy businesses are engaged in a platform business model in which they generate value via their contribution to (i), by innovating new systems to carry out transactions swiftly and efficiently between participants, and they benefit from network effects (ii) which allow them to capture increasing value (profit) as long as the combined price of the participant's offer plus the platform fee is enticing to consumers attracted by the size of the market (See Russo & Stasi, this issue; also see Baden-Fuller & Haefliger, 2013). This business model is not fundamentally new, closely resembling the physical swap-meet business model which pre-dates the internet. Digital networked communication further enables sharing economy businesses to decentralise the exchange (both in time and space), benefiting from indirect network effects and economies of scale.

Although peer-to-peer networks enable communication and exchange, they present a risk to platform operators: there is little to stop new collectives from forming around cheap and widely-available matchmaking tools. Commercial sharing platforms must constantly seek to reduce transaction costs between participants and customers while also ensuring the aggregated offer is competitive. Paradoxically, sharing economy businesses are incentivised to keep participants (sharers) from communicating with one another, as this could provide a basis for collective action or the emergence of competing services. This logic runs counter to traditionally sustainable means of governing common-pool resources, where close ties and communication between providers and appropriators are crucial to sustaining governance (Ostrom, 1990).

The business model logic of the commercial sharing economy helps to explain cognitive dissonance in definitions which seem alien from everyday experiences of 'sharing' (in which, for example, community ties are strengthened via repeat interaction). Sharing economy businesses are aggregated but not necessarily collective. The mutuality fostered by sharing economy platforms is that of membership in a market, not shared possession of a good (See Belk, 2010: 79). We suggest that for sharing economy platforms like Airbnb and Uber, the shared possession which constitutes the commons is not the softness of the beds or the cleanliness of the taxis, but membership itself (who gets to drive, who gets to ride, etc.). This may explain preoccupation with self-regulatory rating systems rather than external controls on the quality of goods or public interest concerns.

One of the dangers posed by the sharing economy is that regulators and citizens confuse sharing economy goods with public or semi-public goods. Public goods are non-excludable, and are therefore 'shared' among users by default. As a result of non-excludability, public goods are frequently under-produced by society, making it a desirable aim of regulators to provide them. Sharing economy goods are used by many but excludable, making them more like club goods (Buchanan, 1965; Fremstad, 2016). Sharing economy services may optimise the use of a durable good or an underemployed worker by making them available to more consumers, but those who cannot pay are excluded from use. Importantly, the algorithms, trademarks and technologies that make up sharing economy platforms themselves are private goods, protected by corporate secrecy, contract and intellectual property rights.

Regulatory Challenges

The changes in social and economic relations implicated by the sharing economy highlighted above have generated particular regulatory challenges. These include issues related to working conditions, trust, risk, liability and individual agency.

Labour / working conditions

One claim made by platform operators is that participants are not 'employees' but something else, like 'micro-entrepreneurs' (Schor et al., 2015; Rogers, 2016). Participants contribute freely to the common pool and can withdraw their offer at any time, so in that sense, they are not employees (companies like Airbnb and Lyft have their own, actual employees who manage the platforms and try to extend the territorial reach of the brand). However, due to precariousness introduced by global systemic crises, sharing economy activity could substitute for what feels like 'work' for many who participate (Cherry, 2016; Walker, 2015). In the absence of traditional permanent employment, sharing economy gig work may constitute a larger proportion of income for some participants. And from the point of view of customers of services like TaskRabbit or Fiverr, the services offered are equivalent to labour. As highlighted in this literature, a major outcome of the change in relationship between worker and employer in the sharing economy is that participants are exposed to greater risk, reduced benefits and lower job security. Consequently regulation may be desirable to protect workers rights and well-being (De Stefano, 2016).

Trust

With reduced social ties compared to other kinds of shared commons, a central regulatory concern for sharing economy services is trust between participants. Relative anonymity and substitutability across the range of offers means that buyers and sellers typically have less information than they would in a traditional exchange. As a response many sharing economy platforms have introduced rating systems (effectively distributing part of the cost of regulating the platform to members). User ratings are problematic in a number of ways: (i) their capacity to be manipulated by dishonest or malicious participants (Lee, 2015) (ii) related, the lack of transparency in the way ratings are assigned, which could conceal bias on the part of the commercial platform, (iii) their simplicity as single-digit reporting devices, masking other important contextual information (Parigi et al, 2013); (iv) alternatively their intrusion into private aspects of participants' lives and disciplinary function. Even assuming that user rating systems can be well-defended from malicious attack and do not mask systemic biases introduced by commercial interests, the removal of traditional commercial parties from exchanges means that those responsibilities must be displaced elsewhere. The trust represented in user ratings might be significant, but the risk is disproportionately borne by individual participants.

Risk and liability

In crowdworking platforms, considerable legal liability is displaced to participants and users themselves. For example Lyft, Uber and similar platforms require that participants have their own driver's licence and insurance. Requirements for criminal records checks and other status checks vary between countries and companies. For Airbnb, home insurance needs to be provided by individual participants. Similarly, there are no health and safety inspections and although, for example, Airbnb 'encourages' hosts to install smoke or carbon monoxide gas detectors they do not require proof for this. Also, there are no requirements to provide a clean criminal record for hosts or guests and, potentially, violent offenders could be host or guests (Airbnb, 2016a; 2016b). This poses obvious risks to both workers and customers. Further to this, there is limited clarity on how the continued status of permits, insurance, and qualifications are updated, monitored or maintained.[3]

This shift from corporate to private responsibility also has implications for the provision for diverse groups in society. It becomes the prerogative of individual service provider whether to provide adequate wheelchair access to Airbnb rooms, or for ride-sharing drivers to cover rural areas or cater for children, as described in Leiren and Aarhaug's article (2016, this issue). All of these factors have obvious public interest implications that have not yet been adequately addressed, either by the platforms themselves or by national legislators.

Agency

Related closely to the above, the status of individual and community agency in the sharing economy has been raised by a number of academic commentators (Rahman, 2015). There are two dimensions to these critiques. Firstly, individual participants in sharing economy networks are limited in their choice about who to transact with and how. Platforms are standardised and anonymised (to take advantage of the efficiencies of technological convergence discussed above). Prices are normally constrained by platform operators and can sometimes be altered by algorithms (e.g. surge pricing) over which participants have little control. With the presence of network effects and in the absence of competition (or portability) between services, participants may find themselves locked into a single platform and subject to unfavourable conditions. Secondly, the ability of communities to impose national or local regulation on sharing economy platforms is reduced due to their novelty, their reliance on non-transparent algorithmic systems and their global reach. In the case of Uber and other ride-sharing applications, one outcome has been that certain municipalities have chosen to outright ban the services from operating, rather than be able to reach an agreement with the platform satisfying the local regulatory context.

Contributions to this Special Issue

Each contribution to this special issue provides a lens on economic and social dimensions of sharing economy practice. Articles are focused on issues of concern rather than individual case studies of platforms. The issues of concern covered by the contributions in this issue are the ontological status of shared goods, the conditions of crowdworking, regulation of trust between strangers, definition of relevant markets for competition regulation and European media policy concerns.

As discussed above, some commercial sharing economy platforms have linked their brands to affectively meaningful offline analogues (e.g., Bed and Breakfast accommodation or informal ride-shares). The ontological status of goods transacted in the sharing economy has implications for how they should be regulated. A central concern for research on the sharing economy is the extent to which the market which is virtualised through peer-to-peer communication rivals other markets constrained by geography and other factors. What features does Airbnb share with a traditional bed-and-breakfast? To what extent can Uber's service be compared to the licensed taxi driving profession? The contribution by Merethe Dotterud Leiren and Jørgen Aarhaug shows that the difference between taxi and non-taxi is not simply a semantic trick to evade classification and resultant regulation. Rather, as the authors demonstrate through interviews with providers on both sides of the divide, the 'taxi' signifies a range of professional, communitarian and public interest effects which are not present or are altered in the virtual taxi service brought to life by sharing economy platforms.

In their contribution, Ayad Al-Ani and Stefan Stumpp provide a typology of P2P crowdworking platforms. These range from anonymised platforms catering to efficiencies of scale in unskilled work such as Amazon's Mechanical Turk, to crowdsourcing platforms offering efficiencies of scope such as InnoCentive. Employment arrangements may be flexible or more formalised and regular, depending on the nature of the work. The authors report on results of a new survey conducted with crowdworkers on the international platform *jovoto*, measuring workers' motivations and concerns. Supported by these data, the authors explore whether existing regulatory frameworks are relevant for workers in the sharing economy or whether organisations like trade unions could potentially play a role in safeguarding their rights. A key finding is that participants report strong intrinsic motivations for participation: 'learning' and 'fun' are invoked more frequently than 'money' by the sample of creative crowdworkers.

Examining trust in online exchange of piratical material, Roberto Tietzmann and Liana Gross Furini provide an empirical window on anonymous, commons-based peer production in a setting where there is no commercial platform intermediary. The authors analyse the way that community consensus formed around naming conventions on a piratical file-sharing website. Although trust between participants is assumed to be low in anonymous, online communities, particularly when illegal infringement is involved, this research unearths incentives and mechanisms by which stable and sustainable practices are formed. The paper offers key insights for sharing economy researchers, offering new data on the rate of cooperative and non-cooperative behaviour under adverse conditions. These insights point the way toward future research to assess and improve trust mechanisms in more formal sharing economy settings, which often rely on peer-to-peer monitoring (ratings) and the possibility of sanctions by the platform provider. In conditions where those mechanisms are unavailable or inappropriate, other commons-based norms may offer alternatives to coordination.

Considering sharing economy platforms from a competition law perspective, Francesco Russo and Maria Luisa Stasi argue in their paper for a more systematic definition of relevant markets covered by sharing economy platforms. The authors suggest that particularly in the case of two-sided markets characterised by network effects, competition authorities should consider not only disruption on traditional markets (for example taxis or hotels), but should examine competition between platforms where offers are supplied. Specifying their relationship to existing markets in order to effectively regulate their new services and markets within current legislative frameworks. Approaching the issue from a legal perspective, Russo and Stasi argue in their paper for the necessity of defining the markets covered by the sharing economy and their relationship to existing markets in order to effectively regulate their new services within current legislative frameworks. In sharing economies where network effects play a key role, competition law becomes particularly pertinent.

Exploring European media policy in the making, Ibrus and Rohn's paper centres on the traditional media industry and the evolution of the European Union's Audiovisual Media Services Directive (AVMSD). Ibrus and Rohn demonstrate how defining what a media company *is* and how production and distribution are understood, becomes crucial for effective regulation, especially when seeking to legislate for diverse new services and platforms in the media industries. In their paper, the authors explore the implications of including online video sharing platforms in the proposed AVMSD. Video sharing platforms, and in particular YouTube increasingly operate like broadcasters and distributors, with multiple channels and premium ad-free subscription options (such as YouTube Red). Yet, where VOD services like Netflix and Amazon Prime are included in the legalisation by the AVMSD, video sharing platforms are currently *not* regulated by the AVMSD but fall under the eCommerce Directive.4Ibrus and Rohn argue that further inclusion of transnational sharing platforms like YouTube in the newly proposed AVMSD (proposed on 25 May 2016) would undermine the AVMSD legislative power. The pooled, aggregated offer of user-generated content on services like YouTube challenges traditional and existing broadcast regulation, precisely because it is user-generated, crowdsourced and shared. Including these platforms in the Directive effectively undermines the protection of European production and content quotas - the very quotas that the new AVMSD directive is set out to safeguard.

Conclusions

By 2025 the sharing economy is expected to generate 335 billion USD in global revenue according to PricewaterhouseCoopers estimates.[5] It will permeate a wide and diverse range of service industries and sectors, from finance, transport, accommodation, media, and secretarial services to creative production and software.

This will impact the composition and constitution of new and established industries, the production of goods and services, the conditions of workers and the customers and users. Consequently it affects policy on all these levels. The collection of papers in this issue of *Internet Policy Review* explore some of the main policy implications, shortcomings and needs in this multifaceted, complex and evolving landscape. The sharing economy is a growing area of productivity, innovation and industry, but maybe also a growing concern. In all the papers in this issue the authors note the dissonance between the connotations and ideals of 'sharing' and the ways these practices play out in a market context where the emphasis is very much on 'economy'.

As a consequence, approaches to studying the sharing economy will need to take account of social as well as economic aspects. The mutuality implied by shared membership in aggregated platforms invites sociological precision. What are the personal motivations, group dynamics, and social norms that govern membership and breathe life into these markets? Importantly, how are the costs and benefits of mutuality shared between members and platform operators? Economic questions concern not only the effects of sharing economy practices for established industries and society as a whole (these will continue to be important). We also need to better understand the economic relations between participants in different configurations of the sharing economy and competitive dynamics between platform service providers and new entrants.

As it grows in size and scope, the sharing economy will undoubtedly attract further attention from policy studies researchers. Throughout the contributions to this special issue there is an implicit - and sometimes explicit - movement towards self-organisation, regulation and legislation. This drive is evident across communities; from supposedly unregulated and anarchic pirate sites as described by Tietzmann and Furini to cross-territory European Union media regulation, as discussed by Ibrus and Rohn. This regulatory impulse exists alongside market transactions and exchanges which take place on these platforms. Discussion around the policy implications, requirements and needs in relation to the sharing economy have just begun.

References

Airbnb (2016a). 'I'm a host. Am I required to have a smoke and CO detector installed?' Available at: https://www.Airbnb.co.uk/help/article/515/i-m-a-host—am-i-required-to -have-a-smoke-and-co-detector-installed?topic=359 (Accessed on 10/06/2016).

Airbnb (2016b). 'What legal and regulatory issues should I consider before hosting on Airbnb?' Available at: https://www.Airbnb.co.uk/help/article/376/what-legal-and -regulatory-issues-should-i-consider-before-hosting-on-Airbnb?topic=197 (Accessed on 10/06/2016).

Baden-Fuller, C., & Haefliger, S. (2013). *Business models and technological innovation. Long range planning*, 46(6), 419-426.

Baldia, S. (2013). The Transaction Cost Problem in International Intellectual Property Exchange and Innovation Markets. *Northwestern Journal of International Law and Business*, 34(1), 1-52.

Barbrook, R. (1998). The hi-tech gift economy. First monday, 3(12). Available at: http:// firstmonday.org/ojs/index.php/fm/article/view/631/552Levine (Accessed on 10/06/2016).

Barta, K., & Neff, G. (2016). Technologies for Sharing: lessons from Quantified Self about the political economy of platforms. *Information, Communication and Society*, 19(4), 518-531.

Belk, R. (2010). Sharing. *Journal of Consumer Research*, 36(5), 715-734.

Belk, R. (2014). You are what you can access: Sharing and collaborative consumption online. *Journal of Business Research*, 67(8), 1595-1600.

Benkler, Y. (2004). Sharing nicely: On shareable goods and the emergence of sharing as a modality of economic production. *Yale Law Journal*, 114, 273-358.

Benkler Y (2006). *The Wealth of Networks*. New Haven and London: Yale University Press.

Botsman, R. (2013). The Sharing Economy Lacks a Shared Definition. Available at: http://www.collaborativeconsumption.com/2013/11/22/the-sharing-economy-lacks-a-shared-definition/ (Accessed on 19/07/2016).

Buchanan, J. M. (1965). An economic theory of clubs. *Economica*, 32(125), 1-14.

Cheng, D. (2014). Is sharing really caring? A nuanced introduction to the peer economy. Report of the Open Society Foundation Future of Work Inquiry.

Cherry, M. A. (2016). Beyond Misclassification: The Digital Transformation of Work. Comparative Labor Law & Policy Journal, 37(3). Accessed online: http://papers.ssrn.com/sol3/papers.cfm?abstract_id=2734288

De Stefano, V. (2016). The Rise of the "Just-in-Time Workforce": On-Demand Work, Crowd Work and Labour Protection in the "Gig-Economy". *Comparative Labor Law & Policy Journal*, 37(3). Accessed online: http://papers.ssrn.com/sol3/papers.cfm?abstract_id=2682602

Eckhardt, GM & Bardhi, F (2015). The Sharing Economy Isn't About Sharing At All. *Harvard Business Review*. January 28, 2015. Accessed online: https://hbr.org/2015/01/the-sharing-economy-isnt-about-sharing-at-all

Erickson, K. (2015). *Topological London*. In I. Franklin, H. Chignell & K. Skoog (eds.) Regional Aesthetics: *Mapping UK Media Cultures*. London: Palgrave.

European Commission (2016). A Fact sheet. European agenda for the collaborative economy. Available at: http://europa.eu/rapid/press-release_MEMO-16-2002_en.htm (Accessed on 18/07/2016).

Fremstad, A. (2016). Sticky Norms, Endogenous Preferences, and Shareable Goods. *Review of Social Economy*, 74(2) 194-214.

Jenkins, H. (2004). The cultural logic of media convergence. *International journal of cultural studies*, 7(1), 33-43.

Lee, C.W. (2015). The Sharer's Gently-Used Clothes. In Juliet B. Schor J., Edward T. Walker E.T., Lee C., Parigi P & Cook K., Viewpoints. On the Sharing Economy. *Contexts*, 14(1), 12-19.

Lessig, L. (2008). *Remix: Making art and commerce thrive in the hybrid economy*. Penguin

Lury, C. (2015). The Sociality of Sharing. Conference Proceedings. Available at: http://www.ce-cp.org/2015/09/the-sociality-of-sharing-university-of-warwick-23-sept-2015/ (Accessed on 10/06/2016).

Mollick E. (2014). The dynamics of crowdfunding: An exploratory study. *Journal of Business Venturing* 29(1), 1–16.

Newsnight (2016). BBC2. 02/06/2016. Available at: https://www.youtube.com/watch?v=m5P9bpj54IY (Accessed on 10/06/2016).

Nicholson N. (1998). How hardwired is human behavior? *Harvard Business Review*, 76, 134-147.

Ostrom, E. (1990). *Governing the Commons: The Evolution of Institutions for Collective Action*. New York: Cambridge University Press.

Ostrom, E., & Gardner, R. (1993). Coping with asymmetries in the commons: Self-governing irrigation systems can work. *The Journal of Economic Perspectives*, 7(4), 93-112.

Parigi, P., Dakhlallah, D., Corten, R., & Cook, K. (2013). A Community of Strangers: The Dis-Embedding of Social Ties. PloS one, 8(7), 67388.

Pew Research Centre (2016). Shared, Collaborative and On Demand: The New Digital Economy. Report. Avaliable at: http://www.pewinternet.org/2016/05/19/the-new-digital-economy/ (Accessed 10/06/2016).

Phipps, Lauren F. (2015). "A Give and A Take": Lived Experiences in a Real Sharing Economy. Pitzer Senior Theses. Paper 61. Available at: http://scholarship.claremont.edu/pitzer_theses/61 (Accessed on 10/06/2016).

Rahman, K. S. (2015). Curbing the New Corporate Power. Boston Review, May 4 2015. Available at: http://bostonreview.net/forum/k-sabeel-rahman-curbing-new-corporate-power (Accessed on 10/06/2016).

Rogers, B. (2016). Employment Rights in the Platform Economy: Getting Back to Basics. *Harvard Law & Policy Review*, 10(2), 480-519.

Schor, J. B., Walker, E. T., Lee, C. W., Parigi, P., & Cook, K. (2015). On the Sharing Economy. *Contexts*, 14(1), 12-19.

Sørensen, I. E. (2015). Go Crowdfund Yourself. In Geert Lovink, Nathaniel Tkacz & Patricia de Vries (eds.), The Moneylab Reader. An Intervention in the Digital Economy. Amsterdam: Institute for Networked Cultures, 268-280.

Tomasello M, Carpenter M, Call J, Behne T, and Moll H (2005). Understanding and sharing intentions: The origins of cultural cognition. *Behavioral and Brain Sciences* 28(5), 675–735.

Walker, E.T. (2015). Beyond the rhetoric of the sharing economy. In Juliet B. Schor J., Edward T. Walker E.T., Lee C., Parigi P & Cook K., Viewpoints. On the Sharing Economy. Contexts, 14(1), 12-19.

Van Dijck J. (2013). *The Culture of Connectivity*. Oxford: Oxford University Press.

The World Wide Web Foundation (2016). The History of the Web. Available at: http://webfoundation.org/about/vision/history-of-the-web/ (Accesed on 10/6/2016).

Footnotes

1. For example, in March 2015, the Higher Regional Court of Frankfurt ruled against Uber and upheld a ban in Germany of the UberPOP service. See LG Frankfurt, docket no. 3-08 O 136/14. The courts in Spain have referred 4 questions to the Court of Justice of the European Union (CJEU) asking for clarification of the status of Uber as a transport service or an information society service. See Asociación Professional Elite Taxi, Case C-434/15. Similar cases are currently before the courts in Denmark in 2016.

2. Baldia (2013) summarises transaction costs as the 'search costs, bargaining costs, and enforcement costs of entering into a transaction' between parties. In the context of the current sharing economy, lowering transaction costs is achieved through automated, geolocative matchmaking, standardisation of offers and instant electronic payment, among other features.

3. Corporate responsibility can be shifted to individual workers and the providers of this service. Phipps (2015) describes how a traffic accident involving an Uber car was deemed the responsibility of the driver and not the company and only after several cases of rape were reported in the global press did a clean criminal record become a requirement for drivers of Uber cars.

4. The newly proposed AVMSD does not include video sharing platforms in its definition of providers of 'TV-like' services and therefore not is its legislation, but it does propose to regulate video sharing platforms in respect to protection of children.

5. See PricewaterhouseCoopers (2015) The sharing economy - sizing the revenue opportunity Accessed online: http://www.pwc.com/gx/en/about/global-annual-review-2015/colliding-megatrends/the-sharing-economy.html

> "As services and software converge, public officials must enhance their technical skills and work with the private sector to ensure market fairness and efficiency."

Regulation of the Sharing Economy Is Necessary

Ayesha Khanna and Parag Khanna

In the following viewpoint, Ayesha Khanna and Parag Khanna explore the sharing economy's effects on businesses, both in terms of how consumers benefit and how business owners benefit, while addressing entrepreneurialism and technological connectivity. The authors argue that, although the sharing economy may be a labor disruptor, eventual regulation will have the effect of boosting the jobs market and the economy. Ayesha Khanna, CEO of Technology Quotient, an education and skills development company, is co-author of Hybrid Reality: Thriving in the Emerging Human-Technology Civilization. *Parag Khanna, Senior Fellow at the New America Foundation and a member of the World Economic Forum's Global Agenda Council on Geo-economics, is the author of* The Second World, How to Run the World, *and co-author of* Hybrid Reality: Thriving in the Emerging Human-Technology Civilization.

"How Should We Regulate the Sharing Economy?" by Parag Khanna, World Economic Forum, September 29, 2014. Reprinted by permission.

As you read, consider the following questions:

1. According to the viewpoint, how does the sharing economy empower individuals?
2. According to the viewpoint, in 2014, what sporting event in Brazil opened the door for an immediate increase in use of home-sharing websites?
3. According to the authors, what are nano-workers?

The increasing ability of people to exchange goods, services and labour directly, via online platforms, is transforming how modern economies operate. But to ensure that the rise of the "sharing economy" works efficiently and improves conditions for all parties, some regulation is needed.

People can now circumvent many traditional service businesses. They can share transport, using Uber, Lyft, or RelayRides; provide accommodation through Airbnb; tender household chores via TaskRabbit, Fiverr, or Mechanical Turk; and arrange their grocery deliveries using Favor and Instacart. Similarly, crowdfunding platforms, such as Kickstarter and Lending Club, allow start-ups to raise grants, loans or investment from the general population, rather than relying on a financial intermediary.

By cutting out the middleman, these online platforms empower individuals, reduce transaction costs and create a more inclusive economy. But their evolution is far from straightforward, and many such services will require careful regulation if they are to flourish – as protests and court rulings in Europe against Uber demonstrate.

One reason why Uber and other sharing economy pioneers are so disruptive is that they represent a highly efficient form of peer-to-peer capitalism. Buyers and sellers can agree directly on the price of every transaction, and business reputations depend on transparent customer feedback, generating continuous pressure to improve performance.

The sharing economy also boosts entrepreneurship, as people see new ways to fill gaps in the market. What began as a simple way

REGULATION'S EFFECT ON THE INDUSTRIES WITHIN THE SHARING ECONOMY

Regulation of Internet-facilitated sharing has a standing history. Napster demonstrated how peer-to-peer sharing could wreak havoc on institutions, and even entire industries. Craigslist is still a buy-at-your-own-risk platform. And today, ride-sharing services like Uber–where black-car drivers act like on-demand taxis–has come under fire for operating in gray areas of legality. Airbnb has faced regulatory challenges at the municipal level in San Francisco and New York, and the California Public Utilities Commission issued a cease-and-desist warning to Lyft and SideCar, two popular ridesharing services based in San Francisco.

The regulatory instinct is to resist new forms of economic exchange to protect both buyers and sellers from fraud or danger. But beyond the questions of trust and reputation, regulators and investors alike are wondering: Does it slow down construction if we use Airbnb instead of hotels? Does it slow down Detroit manufacturing if we share cars and rides instead of buying new ones? Does increasing productivity from existing resources hinder economic growth?

for households to boost incomes – by renting out one's apartment or car – has become a formidable disruptive force. *Forbes* magazine estimates that the sharing economy's 2013 revenues topped $3.5 billion. During the 2014 soccer World Cup in Brazil, a country with a chronic shortage of hotel rooms, more than 100,000 people used home-sharing websites to find accommodation.

The opportunity to buy or sell has also become much more inclusive: half of Airbnb hosts in the United States have low to moderate incomes, and 90% of hosts globally rent their primary residence.

Several cities have recognized the benefits to be gained from promoting a sharing economy. Seattle, for example, has deregulated its transportation and hospitality sectors, challenging the city's taxi and hotel monopolies.

But economic change of this magnitude inevitably has its opponents, some with legitimate concerns. Do peer-to-peer businesses undercut incumbents by not paying similar taxes? Are such businesses – flush with venture capital – running their operations at a loss in order to capture market share? And should these firms be allowed to access telecoms data to learn about customers' habits and movements, thus giving them an unfair advantage?

Some firms have set their own operating standards. TaskRabbit, which subcontracts household jobs like assembling Ikea furniture, requires participants to pay a minimum wage, and has launched an insurance scheme to protect its US workers. On the other hand, technology platforms that use "algorithmic scheduling" to align workers' shifts and hours with business cycles automatically, continue to disrupt family life and cause unnecessary stress. Policymakers need to stay ahead of these sharing economy trends.

As services and software converge, public officials must enhance their technical skills and work with the private sector to ensure market fairness and efficiency. For example, they must prevent the manipulation of reviews and other practices that mislead consumers trying to assess the quality of a company's service. Airbnb and the online travel agent Expedia allow reviews only by customers who have actually used their services; that could become a regulatory norm throughout the sharing economy.

Governments also have a broader role to play. As more people adopt "portfolio careers" – relying on several sources of income, rather than a single job – it becomes harder to collect and analyze labour market data. Governments will need new accounting and reporting standards to calculate wages, forecast incomes and categorize workers within the growing ranks of the self-employed. Such standards, coupled with data-sharing guidelines, will help determine when, and how much, to tax sharing economy transactions.

None of this will be easy. Though self-employment and part-time labour are hardly new, the sharing economy is different, because it allows freelancers to become "nano-workers," shifting among employers not just monthly or even weekly, but several times a day. As US and European unemployment rates remain high and wages stagnate, people increasingly rely on such diverse income streams. Today, almost 27 million Americans survive on part-time and project-based incomes.

With nearly half of all services jobs in the OECD at risk of automation, the sharing economy can smooth the disruption caused to displaced workers as they upgrade their skills. Indeed, sharing-economy data can help governments identify those workers at greatest risk and support their retraining.

The sharing economy reflects the convergence of entrepreneurialism and technological connectivity. Taxi drivers and hotel owners may feel threatened, but the sharing economy has the potential to increase and redistribute earnings in cities that are already struggling with poverty and inequality. Those who are displaced will have far better prospects in the more prosperous and inclusive environment that the sharing economy promises to create.

> *"It is time we matured along with the marketplace and adopted a new word–one that provides less cover for companies that are neither very transparent nor collaborative."*

Retire the Word "Sharing"

Augie Ray

In the following viewpoint, Augie Ray addresses the shift from associations with the word "sharing" for many companies considered to be integral parts of the sharing economy. He goes on to argue that many of these companies weren't actually sharing anything in the first place. The author suggests, instead, the use of the word "leverage" to describe the business models utilized by companies including Uber and Airbnb. Ray is the research director of customer experience for Gartner and runs the blog experiencetheblog.com.

As you read, consider the following questions:

1. According to the author, how relevant is the term "sharing economy"?
2. According to the viewpoint, what happened on the ride-sharing scene in Austin, Texas?
3. Before suggesting "leverage economy," what are a few of the terms the author says will not work in the contexts described?

Let me start by saying that I am a customer and fan of the services offered by Uber (took a ride Monday!), Airbnb (recently booked a family member into a nearby property) and other so-called "sharing" companies. In fact, just this week I gave a presentation about customer experience in which I cited Uber as an example of what brands can achieve with customer-centric product and service experiences. So, I say this as a fan and not as someone who is either anti-tech or anti-innovation: The time has come for companies in the space to stop hiding behind the "sharing economy" label and to improve collaboration with all concerned parties. Failing to do so puts these companies at risk as the industry, customer relationships, and regulations mature.

A year ago, I mounted a passionate defense of the term "sharing economy." At the time, I argued that the word "sharing" was appropriate given these business models facilitate the mutual consumption of assets in contrast to traditional individual ownership and consumption. While this is still true, I cannot shake the feeling that companies have gotten a lot of PR and are camouflaging risky corporate practices thanks to the humanist adjectives they use, including "sharing," "collaborative," "trusted community marketplaces," "the crowd" and "connected." Who can be opposed to those ideas? It'd be like hating motherhood and apple pie!

The problem is that few of these "collaborative" companies are, well, collaborative. For a while, this was easy to overlook, because many consumers agree that some of the regulations these companies flouted were unpopular and, arguably, unnecessary. For example, Uber bypasses municipal safety regulations in many cities, and most of us don't care because we feel safer in an Uber than a taxi. (On my last taxi trip, the driver exceeded the speed limit by 25 mph and barreled through a late yellow light near to a phone-distracted pedestrian, and I reached for my phone to give a bad review only to realize I could not.)

Because we agree some codes are outdated and appreciate the much stronger customer experience offered by the startups, it has been easy to disregard how these companies unilaterally pick which rules they like and which they do not. Laws that shield the companies from unfair practices or protect their intellectual property–yes, please! Laws requiring they follow standard background checks or adhere to local rental ordinances–hey man, can't you see we're trying to innovate here!?

But it is getting harder to ignore the dangers of self-determined laws and regulations. After all, while we give a wink and a nod to Uber snubbing livery laws, do we want the manufacturing plant in our town deciding which environmental standards they'll ignore or food companies to go maverick on safety codes?

As citizens, we all are part of the greatest collaborative platform of all–no, not Uber or Airbnb but democracy. If people don't like certain laws, they can petition their lawmakers to change them; if citizens are not satisfied with their elected officials' response, they can mount a recall or campaign for their defeat. Unless we want companies to set their own laws based on what is best for stockholders (or a handful of VC investors hungry for rapid and sizeable returns), then we must question the green light we give to sharing economy firms to pick the laws they deem worthy.

It seems that green light may be turning yellow. Los Angeles charged a handful of landlords with illegally evicting tenants to convert their units to short-term rentals. The New York State legislature has passed a law that would ban Airbnb users from listing some short-term rentals. Chicago just implemented new (relatively mild) rules for Airbnb. San Francisco's Board of Supervisors unanimously passed a law requiring Airbnb hosts to register with the city. And Austin residents rejected a plan to allow Uber and Lyft to self-regulate.

In response to the new regulations, the sharing companies and their supporters have too often returned to the same old scripts. They accuse officials of being in the pockets of traditional companies. They label new laws as anti-consumer (even as consumers are asking for them). And they accuse officials of being opposed to innovation. In short, these companies ignore that their industry is maturing and many stakeholders are now asking for actions to ensure safety, equitable tax collection, a level playing field for all players, affordable housing availability, and fair rules that protect residents living adjacent to high-traffic, unlicensed hotels.

The reaction to the ride-hailing situation in Austin provides a great example. I have seen tech leaders repeatedly declare that Austin "kicked out Uber and Lyft," which is a substantially misleading perspective that demonstrates the biases and risks at play. Austin held a referendum in which 55,000 people voted–17% of the registered voters in Travis County–and despite an $8 million lobbying effort by Uber and Lyft, Proposition 1 failed by a 12-point margin. Because they didn't get their way, Uber and Lyft took their bat and ball and left the city, leaving thousands of drivers and tens of thousands of riders scrambling to replace their services. Of course, Uber and Lyft can do business (or not) anywhere they wish, but this situation aptly demonstrates the reputation and business risks ahead if sharing economy companies do not collaborate with all parties–not just users of their services but also concerned citizens and officials.

First of all, if you claim to be a consumer-centric, community-based, crowdsourced company but you abandon a market because you do not like the outcome of a free and fair referendum of the people, then you are no longer a consumer-centric, community-based, crowdsourced company; you're just a typical for-profit company striving for financial advantage. Austinites seemed surprised by Uber's and Lyft's unilateral actions. They apparently expected the ride-hailing firms to adapt to their wishes, but for all the trappings of "sharing" and "community," these companies are not benefit corporations, being held accountable for their transparency or positive impact on society. Uber is, in the end, a seven-year-old organization that must justify a valuation greater than the GDP of approximately two-thirds of the nations on earth.

Moreover, the unwillingness of those in Silicon Valley to frame this event in honest terms–not a forced eviction but a willing abandonment of the market–demonstrates an aversion to seeing the very real trends occurring in the marketplace. Many people are no longer willing to look the other way as startups defy the rules. Consumers are anxious for change, but they expect it will come from negotiation and compromise, not ultimatums and blackmail.

Finally, while supporters of the sharing economy cheer the skyrocketing valuations of companies owning almost no fixed assets, the lack of assets is a double-edged sword. It may furnish remarkable levels of financial leverage, but it also means that entry and switching costs are relatively low. When Uber and Lyft abandoned Austin, some young, hungry startups flooded in. If one of them captures drivers' and riders' attention with an identical set of features and a greater willingness to live up to the ideals of the collaborative economy, people's preferences may shift away from the leading ride-hailing services faster than you can say "Myspace."

Which brings me back the question of labels. It is time we matured along with the marketplace and adopted a new word–one that provides less cover for companies that are neither very transparent nor collaborative. There are a variety of other terms people use to describe this space, but none seem quite right. "Peer-to-peer" fails to consider how Uber and Lyft are racing to replace private cars and drivers with a fleet of self-driving vehicles; "on-demand economy" doesn't reflect that some services, such as Airbnb, are not really on-demand; and the "idle economy" works only so long as participants offer unused assets rather than, as is happening, turning currently productive assets (rented apartments) into more productive assets (unlicensed hotels).

My suggestion is that we consider adopting the name "Leverage Economy," which aptly describes what every party is doing. Drivers, hosts and independent contractors leverage their assets, time and skills to make money. Riders, guests and those purchasing services leverage the platforms to save money and gain flexibility over traditional providers. And the platforms themselves are leveraging technology (along with other people's time and assets) to earn profits and exploding valuations from VC investors.

Not only is "leverage economy" a more accurate term, but it may encourage us to think about what is truly happening with this business trend–not selfless sharing and transparent collaboration but an attempt to leverage people and assets to better productivity. That can be a very positive thing for all parties, but it requires us to ask how much leverage we wish to accept. Is it okay for one person to leverage their residence if doing so reduces others' enjoyment of their residences? Is it acceptable for a company to leverage the time of independent contractors who are willing participants, even if their compensation may amount to less than minimum wage? And how much leverage do we want to allow for-profit companies to set their own rules?

The leverage economy can be a good thing for many. It also has the potential to harm others. With greater transparency and collaboration that considers the legitimate concerns and wishes of all parties, we can work together to find the right balance. Companies that fail to do so could find themselves doing irreparable harm to their reputations, customer relationships, and ultimately, their valuations.

The sharing economy is dead. Long live the leverage economy!

Periodical and Internet Sources Bibliography

The following articles have been selected to supplement the diverse views presented in this chapter.

Adam Chandler, "What Should the Sharing Economy Really Be Called?," *The Atlantic,* May 27, 2016. http://www.theatlantic .com/business/archive/2016/05/sharing-economy-airbnb-uber -yada/484505/.

Economist, "All Eyes on the Sharing Economy," TheEconomist.com, March 7, 2013. http://www.economist.com/news/technology -quarterly/21572914-collaborative-consumption-technology -makes-it-easier-people-rent-items.

Economist, "The Rise of the Sharing Economy," TheEconomist.com, March 9, 2013. http://www.economist.com/news /leaders/21573104-internet-everything-hire-rise-sharing -economy.

Editorial Board, "How to Regulate Airbnb and Homesharing," *Los Angeles Times*, June 22, 2016. http://www.latimes.com/opinion /editorials/la-ed-homesharing-law-20160622-snap-story.html.

Robert (RJ) Eskow, "The Sharing Economy Is a Lie: Uber, Ayn Rand and the Truth about Tech and Libertarians," *Salon*, February 1, 2015. http://www.salon.com/2015/02/01/the_sharing_economy _is_a_lie_uber_ayn_rand_and_the_truth_about_tech_and _libertarians/.

Forbes, "Airbnb, Snapgoods, and 12 Pioneer of the Share Economy," Forbes.com. http://www.forbes.com/pictures/eeji45emgkh /airbnb-snapgoods-and-12-more-pioneers-of-the-share -economy/#1b8743e17226.

Steven Greenhouse, "The Whatchamacallit Economy," *New York Times*, December 16, 2016. https://www.nytimes. com/2016/12/16/opinion/the-whatchamacallit-economy.html.

Greg Jericho, "The Dark Side of Uber: Why the Sharing Economy Needs Tougher Rules," *Guardian*, April 17, 2016. https://www .theguardian.com/business/grogonomics/2016/apr/18/uber -airbnb-sharing-economy-tougher-rules-australia.

Aaron Smith, "Shared, Collaborative, and On Demand: The New Digital Economy," Pew Research Center, PewInternet.org, May 19, 2016. http://www.pewinternet.org/2016/05/19/the-new -digital-economy/.

Niam Yaraghi and Shamika Ravi, "The Current and Future State of the Sharing Economy," Brookings.edu, December 29, 2016. https://www.brookings.edu/research/the-current-and-future -state-of-the-sharing-economy/.

OPPOSING
VIEWPOINTS®
SERIES

CHAPTER 2

How Do the Sharing Economy and Conventional Businesses Affect One Another?

Chapter Preface

One of the primary—and critical—factors to consider in any assessment of the sharing economy is the relationship between this relatively new set of businesses (such as Uber and Airbnb) and the conventional versions of each of them (like taxis and hotels). While many aspects of the topic are up for discussion, there is no question as to whether these two halves of what we can call the "service economy whole" affect one another.

Experts and researchers of the sharing economy are quick and consistent in pointing out a need for regulations that apply to everyone in a way that is fair, accessible, and understandable. These regulations ultimately need to be clearly communicated to the public at large.

Questions with seemingly obvious answers, like, "Is Uber even part of the sharing economy?" are asked, and conventions, however newly established they may be, are challenged. From consumer protection, to competitive issues, to privacy practices, big-picture challenges are explored and explained in this chapter.

Some challenges facing the sharing economy with regard to regulation will take time for consumers and businesses alike to fully understand, and even more time for these stakeholders to come to places of agreement. The role of professional organizations offers a prime example of a previously clear-cut element of the world of regulations that now is quite nebulous.

Common themes throughout the chapter include a need for regulation in order to establish legitimacy for the sharing economy among the general public and a reliance on consumer feedback after they use these products and, mostly, services. The regulations proposed by several authors in this chapter include examples and reasons include protection of the service providers, say, the driver or homeowner, to protection of the purchaser, who could be a passenger or apartment renter.

The authors of the viewpoints that follow in this chapter present a collective range of perspectives, and some offer solutions to the conflicts and causes for concern.

> "*The sharing economy must be carefully regulated so that we can fully maximize efficiency gains.*"

Uber and the Taxi Industry Must Find a Middle Ground

Georgios Petropoulos

In the following viewpoint, Georgios Petropoulos covers the conflicts and concerns between the longstanding taxi industry in many cities—both in the United States and in Europe—and the rise of Uber's prevalence in those cities. These points make clear that the need for regulations as Uber grows in metropolitan areas worldwide. Differences in the basic business models between the two are laid out, and the nuances of how Uber's pricing is established as well as how it fluctuates are explained. Petropoulos is a resident fellow at the Brussels-based economic think tank Bruegel. He holds several degrees, including a research master's degree on markets and organizations and a PhD from Toulouse School of Economics.

As you read, consider the following questions:

1. What concept is the basis for Uber's pricing model?
2. In what US city did use of taxis plummet by 65% in the first two years of Uber's presence?
3. What are the primary concerns voiced by European taxi companies that have brought this issue to court?

"Uber and the Economic Impact of Sharing Economy Platforms," by Georgios Petropoulos, Bruegel, February 22, 2016.

The 'sharing economy' matches people who want to share assets online. Rather than buying a power drill that I only need for 15 minutes, for example, I can just rent one from someone else who's not using theirs. Such efficiency gains may come at cost for the traditional economy. Manufacturers of power drills might see profits shrink due to the drop in demand and may even be driven out of the market.

However the costs and benefits associated with sharing economy platforms depend on the business models in place.

Uber is one of the fastest growing startups worldwide, but its rise has led to massive demonstrations by taxi drivers. Courts have banned or restricted Uber's services for engaging in unfair competition with regular taxis. While other ridesharing online platforms like Lyft and Sidecar use similar business models, Uber is at the centre of the debate due to its size and rapid growth worldwide.

In December Uber was valued at $68 billion, having taken just 6 years to surpass the valuation of 100-year-old companies like General Motors and Ford, as well as "traditional" transportation companies like Hertz and Avis[2].

Uber vs. taxis: passengers

Uber connects drivers offering rides and passengers seeking them online. Potential passengers download an app that allows them to request the nearest available Uber car on their smartphone. The company does not own cars, but signs up private drivers willing to provide rides to paying passengers and passes the ride requests directly to them.

Uber sets the price of the ride, and transactions happen through the online platform. 70-80% of each fare goes to the driver and the rest is kept by Uber.

Uber's online platform is user-friendly, and its rates are generally lower than regular taxis[3]. Uber is cheaper in most major American cities, even excluding the taxi driver's tip, as shown in Table 1 and 2.

Side note: Silverstein, 2014, calculates the fares for a sample trip of 5 miles in 10 minutes under car speed of 30MPH with no waiting time. Tables 1 and 2 refer to baseline estimates, without "surge pricing".

TABLE 1 SAMPLE TRIP: 5 MILES, NO IDLING				TABLE 2 ADD 20% TIP TO TAXI TARE		
UBER	TAXI	TAXI/ UBER	CITY	UBER	TAXI + 20% TIP	TAXI/ UBER
17.75	15.50	0.9	New York	17.75	18.60	1.0
15.25	14.20	0.9	Philadelphia	15.25	17.04	1.1
15.05	15.00	1.0	Portland	15.05	18.00	1.2
13.00	13.95	1.1	Cleveland	13.00	16.74	1.3
10.30	11.25	1.1	Dallas	10.30	13.40	1.3
13.25	14.50	1.1	Miami	13.25	17.40	1.3
11.65	13.00	1.1	Indianapolis	11.65	15.60	1.3
11.00	12.50	1.1	Phoenix	11.00	15.00	1.4
12.15	14.25	1.2	Minneapolis	12.15	17.10	1.4
10.75	13.05	1.2	Baltimore	10.75	15.66	1.5
10.20	12.85	1.3	Columbus	10.20	15.42	1.5
10.35	13.75	1.3	Denver	10.35	16.50	1.6
12.30	16.50	1.3	Detroit	12.30	19.80	1.6
11.70	16.00	1.4	Seattle	11.70	19.20	1.6
12.30	17.25	1.4	San Francisco	12.30	20.70	1.7
9.50	14.00	1.5	Chicago	9.50	16.80	1.8
11.10	16.60	1.5	Boston	11.10	19.92	1.8
10.00	15.00	1.5	Atlanta	10.00	18.00	1.8
9.00	13.75	1.5	Houston	9.00	16.50	1.8
11.35	17.80	1.6	San Diego	11.35	21.36	1.9
9.40	16.35	1.7	Los Angeles	9.40	19.62	2.1

SOURCE: *Business Insider.* Fare Sources: Uber, TaxiFareFinder.com

Uber's pricing model is dynamic, changing the price to equalize supply with demand. If there is high demand for rides and few drivers on the road (common at weekends or on national holidays), the price increases.

This motivates more drivers to work, and reduces the number of passengers, as some prefer other modes of transportation (for example regular taxis) if the price is high.

The app informs customers when "surge pricing" takes place, and the price of the increased fare, so there is no asymmetric information.

However the Uber pricing algorithm has raised antitrust concerns regarding whether it facilitates implicit collusion among drivers[4]. Critics point out that when competitors (drivers) agree on a pricing structure rather than competing against each other, this may qualify as price fixing.

Moreover, in many cities, Uber's pricing depends on the speed of the ride. Regular taxis charge riders per mile when moving, and per minute when idling. Uber charges riders per mile and minute whether they're moving or idling. So, Uber prices drop as speed increases, since it is charging simultaneously for the miles and the driving time. As a result, taxis may become a more attractive option during times of traffic (provided that they are available and can be reached).

In comparison to regular taxis, Uber has several advantages beyond lower fares. Instead of waiting in the street or calling a taxi service, passengers can request a car through Uber's online platform and watch the car's progress towards their location.

In addition, transactions are performed electronically (with the exception of India where passengers can pay in cash if they wish) and so passengers can travel without cash or cards.

Users can check the profile of the driver before selecting them and give their own opinion rating after the ride. This makes them feel safer than entering the car of a completely unknown driver. If the average rating of a driver is low, then they are dismissed by Uber.

The impact of Uber on the taxi industry

Uber's success has been detrimental to the traditional taxi industry. Taxis are heavily regulated: rates are fixed and taxis must buy licences to operate. Such licenses are issued rarely, and become more valuable as the urban population grows. In big US cities the price (before Uber's operation) varied between $350,000 and $1,000,000, while in Paris licences cost around 240,000 euros[5].

However Uber has severely reduced the value of licenses, as Uber drivers do not need licenses to enter the market. Licenses no longer grant protection from competition. Taxi drivers are no longer able to sell off their licenses as expected, and they are not financially protected against such sudden devaluations.

In this way Uber's entry has made things much more difficult for taxi drivers. In New York for example, the price of individual licenses dropped from $1 million in 2013 to $700,000-$800,000 in 2015, while in Chicago, they decreased by 33.3%. The asymmetry over the regulatory requirements (buy a taxi license vs. become an Uber driver for free) to enter the business creates unfair competition between the two.

Restrictions on the number of available taxi licenses vary across the world. In New York there are 13.5 taxis (including private hire vehicles) for every 1000 inhabitants, while in London there are 10.8, in Stockholm 7.8 and in Paris only 3.4[6]. The number of issued licenses may be affected by strong taxi lobbies that target high entry barriers, as in Paris and Brussels. Uber's entry into the market has gradually reduced demand for traditional taxis. The number of trips by taxis in New York fell by 8% between 2012 and 2014 (Wallsten, 2015). The trend was even more acute in San Francisco,[7] where use of taxis declined by 65% in the two years after Uber's entry[8].

However, the reported number of complaints per taxi ride in New York decreased after the Uber's entry into the market (Wallsten, 2015[9]), suggesting that taxis unable to respond to Uber's entry by reducing their regulated prices responded by improving their services.

The reported number of complaints per taxi ride in New York decreased after the Uber's entry into the market.

We should note, however, that due to data restrictions, Wallsten is unable to quantify the magnitude of this quality effect of Uber on taxi services. Experience shows that in some cases, taxi unions reacted by modernizing their fleet and launching online apps to reduce search costs for passengers[10].

Uber drivers

The number of Uber drivers has increased exponentially in recent years, as individuals have found Uber a flexible way to top up their income. 61% of Uber drivers in Boston, Chicago, Washington, Los Angeles, New York and San Francisco have another job (Hall and Krueger, 2015).

However, Uber drivers are considered independent contractors, so they are not entitled to the minimum wage, paid vacations or health insurance. Earnings per hour for Uber drivers are higher than the hourly wages of taxi drivers and chauffeurs in Boston, Chicago, Washington, Los Angeles, New York and San Francisco (Hall and Krueger, 2015),[11]but estimated earnings for Uber drivers do not account for costs incurred during the trip but only for Uber fees.

A study by NerdWallet in the same cities estimates that Uber drivers would receive health care benefits worth an average of $5,500 a year, plus thousands more in mileage reimbursement, if the company provided them with the same benefits as its full-time employees[12].

In addition, there have been multiple reported cases of violence of passengers against drivers,[13] who due to their employment status are not eligible to work protection.

Two US courts (in California and Florida) have recently ruled individual Uber drivers are regular employees, and ordered Uber to reimburse them for mileage or pay unemployment benefits. Uber drivers in the UK have filed claims seeking to change their status to employees rather than self-employed contractors[14].

Earnings Per Hour or Hourly Wages

	UBER DRIVER-PARTNERS (EARNINGS PER HOUR)	OES TAXI DRIVERS AND CHAUFFEURS (HOURLY WAGES)
Boston	$20.29	$12.92
Chicago	$16.20	$11.87
Washington, DC	$17.79	$13.10
Los Angeles	$17.11	$13.12
New York	$30.35	$15.17
San Francisco	$25.77	$13.72
Average BSG Survey Uber Markets	$19.19	$12.90

SOURCE: Hall and Krueger (2015)

Competition policy and regulation

Taxi companies in Europe have gone to court, arguing that Uber does not comply with taxi regulations and therefore engages in unfair competition. Uber is now banned or subject to serious restrictions in Belgium, France, Germany, Italy and Spain. Such decisions have intensified the debate around Uber[15].

Former European Commissioner Neelie Kroes even characterized the court decision to ban Uber from Brussels as "crazy" and in favor of a taxi cartel[16].

Regulatory bodies around Europe were not ready for platforms like Uber. Regulators failed to react to the emergence of ride sharing online platforms and revise their price cap restrictions for taxis. Strong taxi lobbies have also made the authorities' work more difficult.

The solution to all this is not to ban Uber, but to regulate it. The unfair competition is the result of the regulatory asymmetry between taxis and online ridesharing companies. Regulators must to establish a framework that enhances the benefits and eliminates the associated costs and risks.

The Sharing Economy in a Nutshell

The rise of "sharing economy" firms is one of leading business stories of the last half-decade. [...] In general, sharing firms either (1) own goods or services that they rent to customers on a short-term basis or (2) create peer-to-peer platforms connecting providers and users for short-term exchanges of goods or services. Unlike previous start-up booms, sharing firms have seldom been in conflict with large technology firms or federal regulators. Instead, their biggest problems have come from city and state politics, where locally-regulated "real economy" competitors and other groups have aggressively fought the sharing newcomers. The taxi industry claims Uber, the leading "ride sharing" firm, enjoys an unfair advantage because it need not purchase medallions or comply with consumer protection or pricing regulations. Hotels and neighborhood groups argue AirBnB, the leading "house sharing" firm, skirts taxes, violates lease terms, uses residentially-zoned property for commercial purposes, and lacks safeguards for guests and operators.

"Like Uber, but For Local Government Policy: The Future of Local Regulation of the 'Shared Economy,'" by Daniel E. Rauch and David Schleicher, Marron Institute of Urban Management, January, 2015.

One approach would be to balance passengers' benefits and the incurred damages by taxi drivers. But such an approach would ignore the dynamic aspects of the competitive game.

The presence of Uber might force the taxi industry to innovate and adopt new technologies to improve their services and survive. Competitive pressure combined with the appropriate regulatory measures can lead to efficiency.

For example, liberalising price regulations could make taxis more competitive, by increasing social benefits further (as the Irish example has shown). The fixed rate of taxi fares was introduced to remove information asymmetries and protect consumers from taxi drivers behaving improperly. If new technologies can prevent such risks, then restrictive price regulation will no longer be necessary.

If taxis are unable to respond to the challenge of Uber, then they will gradually be driven out of the market and Uber will become the dominant player. In this case, potential entrants and smaller competitors would fear abuse of dominance by Uber.

A proper regulatory response should address such concerns. In 2014 members of Uber's New York office were accused of using aggressive sales techniques against their sharing economy competitors Lyft[17] and Gett.[18] This shows that technology can also be used to develop market strategies that damage competition and set entry barriers, without strictly violating competition law.

Given Uber's dynamic pricing policy, passengers can also be hurt when prices are high if there is a lack of alternative operators. If traditional taxis were taken out of the market and other sharing economy firms were unable to enter, there would be limited alternative options besides Uber, especially in cities with poor public transportation.

Authorities should make sure that the market remains open to competitors of Uber, so that passengers are able to switch operators and Uber does not become dominant in the market, as market dominance and monopolies are translated to high prices for passengers.

The future of urban transportation will rely heavily on technologies that facilitate information sharing and reduce asymmetries. It is up to regulatory bodies to certify that the associated efficiency gains will be maximized and distributed in a fair share among all involved parties.

Recommendations

The taxi industry should be more lightly regulated. Current taxi industry regulations aim to protect taxi drivers from competition. The emergence of platforms like Uber makes the market more competitive and benefits consumers through lower prices and better quality services. Liberalisation of the industry may help taxi drivers to compete more effectively with Uber, by improving their services. At the same time, switching costs should be low so that Uber drivers are able to work for multiple companies.

The current employment status of Uber drivers shifts the most of risks towards them. **Uber must adopt a new employment relationship towards its workers**, preserving flexibility over working hours, but also ensuring a safe work environment.

Work protection and insurance would make roles, responsibilities and liabilities distinct and transparent. Increased work protection would also incentivize Uber to run additional background checks and to increase the standards of its operation, for example through well-defined insurance schemes).

Passengers and drivers would no longer be under legal uncertainty about liabilities, reducing potential legal costs.

Collective bargaining should play a greater role. Under its current business model, Uber has all the bargaining power. It fixes the price of the offline service, sets the conditions under which passengers and drivers use the online platform, and markets and negotiates the purchase of the service.

Letting Uber drivers name their fares and compete for passengers could create extra flexibility and benefit consumers.

Regulation must also take into account data privacy issues. Since personal data is involved, data protection authorities must make sure data is safe, in line with the criteria and safeguards that have been established by the Directive 95/46/EC of the European Parliament and the European Council. Data portability should be secured so that users of the Uber platform can move to a competitor platform whenever they want.

International cooperation and harmonization of tax rules is needed to eliminate tax evading strategies. Taxing online platforms has proven problematic. Online platforms, through their subsidiaries, can be taxed in Bermuda for a ride that took place in Italy.

The call for a global tax rule by Piketty (2013)[19] will not only reduce inequality, but could also improve the public finances of many countries. Since traditional local industries cannot use online networks to avoid revenue taxes, such practices can jeopardize a level playing field.

Technology can enable us to move to more efficient ways of transportation which can benefit passengers and society. The sharing economy must be carefully regulated so that we can fully maximize efficiency gains.

We must set the rules of interaction between online ridesharing and traditional firms in order to secure a level playing field. At the same time, we should make sure that a safe work environment is provided, eliminating potential risks for passengers and drivers.

Endnotes

[1] Excellent research assistance by Elena Vaccarino is gratefully acknowledged.

[2] http://www.forbes.com/sites/ellenhuet/2014/06/06/at-18-2-billion-uber-is-worth-more-than-hertz-united-airlines/#1e39135439d6

[3] http://www.businessinsider.com/uber-vs-taxi-pricing-by-city-2014-10?IR=T

[4] See Gata (2015), "The Sharing Economy, Competition and Regulation". Competition Policy International.

[5] http://business.lesechos.fr/entrepreneurs/idees-de-business/10033234-taxis-contre-vtc-la-drole-de-guerre-sur-un-marche-tres-convoite-55731.php

[6] See Uber's October 2015 mobility case study for Paris.

[7] http://bruegel.org/2014/09/the-economics-of-uber/

[8] http://bruegel.org/2014/09/the-economics-of-uber/

[9] See Scott Wallsten (2015), " The Competitive effect of the Sharing Economy: How is Uber Changing Taxis?". Technology Policy Institute

[10] http://www.seattletimes.com/seattle-news/seattle-yellow-cab-on-the-comeback-path/, http://www.theatlantic.com/business/archive/2015/07/uber-taxi-drivers-complaints-chicago-newyork/397931/

[11] See Table 6 in Hall and Krueger (2015), "An Analysis of the Labor Market for Uber's Driver-Partners in the United States". Working Papers (Princeton University. Industrial Relations Section).

[12] http://time.com/money/4005662/uber-drivers-earnings-employee-benefits/

[13] http://www.forbes.com/sites/ellenhuet/2015/01/06/workers-compensation-uber-drivers-sharing-economy/#6c50683f4c78

[14] http://www.buzzfeed.com/johanabhuiyan/uber-drivers-in-the-uk-just-filed-an-employee-misclassificat#.ni1ZE83Yg

[15] See Geradin (2015), "Should Uber be Allowed to Compete in Europe? And if so How?". Competition Policy International.

[16] http://ec.europa.eu/archives/commission_2010-2014/kroes/en/content/crazy-court-decision-ban-uber-brussels-show-your-anger.html

[17] http://www.theverge.com/2014/8/26/6067663/this-is-ubers-playbook-for-sabotaging-lyft

[18] https://newsroom.uber.com/statement-on-uber-nyc-driver-outreach/

[19] Thomas Piketty (2013), "Capital in the Twentieth Century". Harvard University Press.

> *"There is a need to reestablish a level playing field, which may call for a revision of those regulatory frameworks, as they may be unsuitable to deal with efficiency enhancing technological changes."*

We Need Offline, Not Digital, Policy for the Online Economy

João E. Gata

In the following viewpoint, João E. Gata looks at the various activities that make up the sharing economy, and offers a few alternate terms and definitions in this area. Gata demonstrates the need for clear-cut regulations, and ones that are not limited to internet-based businesses. He also explores the differences between professional and peer sellers, in the context of whether they are comparable. Gata is the Principal Advisor to the PCA's President's Cabinet. PhD in Economics, University of Minnesota, Twin Cities/USA. He holds a diploma in post-graduate studies in EU Competition Law/King's College, London/UK. He is a professor of economics at the University of Aveiro/Portugal.

"The Sharing Economy, Competition and Regulation", by João E. Gata , Competition Policy International, November 26, 2015. Reprinted by permission.

As you read, consider the following questions:

1. According to the author, what constitutes an on-demand service?
2. According to this viewpoint, what industry recognizes longevity with medallions?
3. According to the author, by what year is the sharing economy expected to surpass $330 billion?

Abstract

The term 'sharing economy' has become an umbrella encompassing different types of economic activities, somewhat informal, though all of them dependent on online platforms that bring together providers of different goods and services and users, and where mutual trust is an essential input as standard and more intrusive regulation is often absent. Involving new governance structures as a response to lower transaction costs, the sharing economy can promote greater efficiency in the use of already existing economic assets and lead to possibly better investment strategies. Besides questioning traditional economic regulation, it may also pose challenges to competition policy, as regarding for example the use of common pricing algorithms. Uber, one instance of the 'sharing economy' when loosely understood, has experienced particularly contentious challenges to its activity in many of the different countries and municipalities where it operates or used to operate. Its activity has challenged long existing transport regulation and the incumbents' long standing presence in different markets. Reestablishing a level playing field may call for a welcoming revision of such regulations without discouraging efficiency enhancing technological changes. This reform process may benefit from well-established strands in economics, namely transaction costs economics and club goods theory, as they may help us to better understand the impact and future developments of the 'sharing economy'.

Introduction

Sharing assets is an old practice in human societies. The so-called "sharing economy" is much more recent, as it involves matching people who want to share assets via online platforms, potentially at a global scale, through the use of personal computers, tablets and smartphones.

The term "sharing economy" may not have a consensual definition and has been used as a catchword encompassing different, but possibly overlapping, types of more or less informal economic activities, though all of them dependent on online platforms and all of them involving new governance structures[2]. In fact, terms such as "sharing economy", "on-demand service" and "collaborative consumption" have been used as close substitutes, or even synonyms[3]. We may follow Botsman (2015) in her attempt, even if not totally successful, to clarify these concepts, by defining "sharing economy" as *an economic system based on sharing underused assets or services, for free or for a fee, directly from individuals*, as is the case of Airbnb or BlaBlaCar[4]. On the other hand, Uber would be classified as an "on-demand service[5], i.e., *a platform that directly matches customer's needs with providers to immediately deliver goods and services*. In this case, no sharing of underused assets may be involved at all[6]. In the case of "collaborative consumption", still according to Botsman, there is a reinvention of traditional market behaviors (such as renting, lending, swapping, sharing, bartering, and gifting) through a technology that takes place in ways and on a scale not possible before the internet. What is common to sharing economies, on-demand services and collaborative consumption is the use of computers, tablets, smartphones as IT devices to easily access goods and services in the real world. For the purpose of this column, let us agree on using the term "sharing economy" as an umbrella for all these different activities[7], as most of the issues that will be addressed here are common to all of them.

Sharing makes sense particularly for items that are expensive to buy and are widely owned by people who do not make full use of them, i.e., do not use them all the time, allowing others to use them in a non-rivalry way[8]. Sharing economies increase economic efficiency as they reduce idleness in the use of already existing assets, and may spur further investment[9].

"Sharing Economies"

Sharing economies involve new forms of production, transaction (mostly spot transactions) and consumption. They may be regarded as examples of "disruptive innovations" in that they compete with traditional ways of producing, distributing and consuming goods and services, through the use of technological innovations such as smartphones, digital content and online distribution that may be considered disruptive[10]. The new forms of production and of (mostly) spot transactions lead us back to the literature on 'markets vs. firms' and how these two alternative forms of organizing economic activity may arise to minimize associated transaction costs[11]. As these types of technological innovations (including the download of apps) reduce transaction costs (e.g., they reduce the costs of dispersion[12], as it is now much cheaper to match the two sides of a market, i.e., they thicken an otherwise too thin a market, thus increasing economic efficiency[13], they facilitate trade: people are able to rely more on (spot, peer-to-peer) markets (in this case, digitalized markets) and less on firms for the production and distribution of goods and services. i.e., on 'markets vs. firms' as two alternative forms of organizing economic activity, we would see "more markets and less firms"[14].

Sharing economies include activities such as: people and pets' accommodation; car-sharing and car-parking; ; boat and bike-sharing; air travel; rental of art works, designer clothes and accessories; start-up financing, peer-to-peer lending, crowdfunding and consumer loans; computer programming;; skill and tool / DIY; marketing and branding. Even if several incumbents operating in these markets may fight this new type of competition, some incumbents are themselves joining in the "sharing economy".

This is the case with e.g., Avis, Daimler, GM, B&Q in the UK, by listing excess capacity (cars, office space, and other durable physical assets) on peer-to-peer rental sites. And they have the advantage of bringing in their solid reputation. Just like what has been happening with online shopping (Walmart and Tesco, for example). They are not necessarily cannibalizing themselves; they want to compete with newcomers and expand their markets[15].

For online platform mediated transactions in the sharing economy to be successful, high enough degrees of coordination and trust have to be guaranteed and maintained over time. As for coordination, and as mentioned above, online platforms allow for easier and better matches between larger numbers of providers and customers: as they reduce the costs of dispersion, it is much cheaper to match the two sides of a market. Concerning trust, for people to be willing to be a part of sharing economies, and in view of economic agents bounded rationality and information asymmetries, they expect that opportunism, hold-up problems, and other contractual hazards are held down to acceptable levels. Among other things, this means being able to rely on internet based reputation systems, possibly of their own design and for their own use, as part of a governance structure that guarantees the existence and attainment of separating equilibria outcomes, where trustworthy people are publicly discriminated from opportunists[16]. In fact, ill-designed internet reputation systems, unable to deliver a high enough level of the public good "trust", can jeopardize the very existence of a sharing economy[17][18].

How significant are "sharing economies"? Figures are hard to come by but PwC has calculated that on a world basis, the sharing economy is currently worth around US$ 13bn, with this value rising to around US$ 335bn by 2025[19], and this just including peer-to-peer accommodation, car sharing, peer-to-peer finance, music, TV and video streaming, and online staffing.[20]

Competition and Regulatory Challenges

What new challenges for competition policy, if any, do sharing economies raise? For example, does the 'Uber pricing algorithm' pose any challenge for antitrust, e.g., does it facilitate some form of collusion or price/behavior parallelism among drivers working with Uber? Is it responsible for the so-called 'Uber prices surges' that has been criticized by Uber customers?[21] When competitors agree on a pricing structure rather than competing against each other, this may qualify as price fixing. If drivers working with Uber are independent contractors and Uber's pricing algorithm they use does not guarantee their prices are determined in an independent fashion, then price fixing may be occurring. To what extent such algorithms are essential for the well-functioning of the platform? In general, one can question to what extent does the increasing use of ever "smarter algorithms" in market transactions, in particular transactions mediated via online platforms, raise competition concerns in light of TFUE article 101, even starting with the proper determination of liability for misconduct and illegal behavior. [22][23]

As for economic regulation, and following Grossman (2015), we can set a contrast between classic economic regulation, when it restricts access to an economic activity to achieve certain public policy goals, e.g., public safety, and a less intrusive economic regulation which relaxes market access restrictions. For a less intrusive regulation to be viable and acceptable, it depends on the success of internet reputation systems which, by using large amounts of real-time data on economic agents participating in sharing economies, can sustain separating equilibria outcomes most of the time, lowering enforcement and accountability costs[24][25]. In fact, moving towards a more decentralized and less intrusive type of regulation, where peer pressure and peer review play such a crucial role, will be less desirable if the information asymmetry between the different economic agents involved in an online platform mediated transaction is too high and difficult to overcome. For example, in the case of credence goods or services, such move may be difficult to justify as any peer review, even in the case of homogenous preferences between peers, will provide me with a noisy signal about the true quality of the good or service. Is this the case with Uber? According to some recent Court rulings in different jurisdictions, which do not necessarily regard Uber as simply an online platform, Uber's activity does pose a risk to customers, which will warrant some form of protection by the State as there is a public security issue at stake.

Another challenge that today's regulators face are the increasingly blurred dividing lines between who is a professional (or dedicated producer/seller) and who is not (i.e., who is a peer seller) when they both offer the same type of goods or services, i.e., when they can coexist and compete with each other[26]. Even if in any given jurisdiction the regulator is able to make a clear distinction between them in each instance, the point is that the number of instances needing clarification may grow very fast and a broad and stable enough distinction may be elusive. Hence, it seems that the "sharing economy" not only has been challenged by existing regulations, but it is itself posing challenging questions on the scope and intent of such regulations. Finally, the challenges posed by sharing economies to the fiscal system are certainly important but their analysis lays beyond the scope of this short note.

The Case of UBER

Together with Airbnb, Uber has occupied a central role in recent academic papers and in specialized news on the "sharing economy"[27]. The way different jurisdictions have responded to the challenge posed by Uber to incumbents illustrates several of the issues raised above. For the most part, these responses have been of a regulatory nature. Drivers operating for Uber are said to be operating without the proper licenses; Uber itself has been regarded as a company operating transport services but doing so without the proper licenses and certificates; public safety issues have also been raised. Moreover, complaints about Uber's "unfair competition" when, it is claimed, there is already an "excess supply of taxi services" (a claim which is hard to reconcile with the very high values taxi medallions achieve in the secondary market, e.g., on online auction platforms such as OLX), have been reflected in decisions by Courts called to rule on the matter in several jurisdictions, sometimes answering requests for an injunction to be issued against Uber's activities. This was the case in Portugal, where Uber had been operating its service Uber Black since July 2014, and UberX since December 2014. Following a complaint by a national association of taxi owners, using most of the arguments mentioned above, a preliminary injunction against Uber was issued by a Court in Lisbon last 24th April 2015, followed by an appeal by Uber and a final decision by this same Court last June 25th, prohibiting Uber's activities in Portugal.

Many of these complaints by incumbents go beyond competition policy, at least as defined in many jurisdictions. However, they have the merit of focusing our attention on the need to revisit the existing regulatory framework on taxi services, which may have outlived its usefulness and whose broadness and intrusiveness may be hard to justify. Another recurrent issue, over which there is already some jurisprudence[28], is on whether drivers contracting with Uber are its employees or operate as independent contractors. As mentioned above, their juridical nature is crucial in helping to determine whether Uber's pricing algorithm can be regarded in any way as facilitating collusion between independent market operators.

Finally, the forceful response of taxi services incumbents to what they regard as Uber's encroachment on their economic activity has a lot to do with the very high values taxi medallions achieve in the secondary market, as mentioned above. The owners of such medallions regard them as an important part of their retirement plan and, as such, will strongly oppose their devaluation following a market liberalization initiative. Taxi services in Ireland were deregulated by a Decision of the Irish High Court in 2000, and affirmed by judicial review in 2001[29]. The High Court also issued three judgments against compensation for the holders of taxi medallions following the deregulation of the sector and the devaluation of such medallions in the secondary market. This is to say, holding a medallion was not considered a property right meriting compensation following its devaluation.

Conclusion

The term "sharing economy" encompasses different types of economic activities, somewhat informal, all of them dependent on online platforms matching providers of different goods and services and their users to an extent greater than ever, and where mutual trust is an essential input in the absence of a standard and more intrusive regulation. The sharing economy promotes greater economic efficiency by allowing a more intensive use of underused economic assets already held by households. The "sharing economy" is rising in value and is set to surpass US$ 330bn by 2025. Airbnb and Uber are possibility its best known examples. Both have raised regulators' concerns, as they challenge long-existing regulatory frameworks, particularly in the case of Uber, and have led to complaints of "unfair competition" by incumbents and, in some cases, to court decisions based on existing regulations. There is a need to reestablish a level playing field, which may call for a revision of those regulatory frameworks, as they may be unsuitable to deal with efficiency enhancing technological changes. The "sharing economy" may also raise some competition issues, as when independent contractors operating on one side of the platform may be using a common pricing algorithm. New regulatory and competition issues may arise as the sharing economy evolves and its characteristics are better understood.

Endnotes

[1] Principal Advisor, Portuguese Competition Authority (PCA/AdC), Lisbon, Portugal. Also member of GOVCOPP, DEGEI, Universidade de Aveiro, Portugal, and Ph.D. in Economics, University of Minnesota, USA & Post Grad Diploma EU Competition Law, King's College, London. The views expressed in this paper are solely my own and do not necessarily represent the views of other people or institutions, unless when explicitly noted.

[2] The study of governance is concerned with the identification, explication and mitigation of all forms of contractual hazards – see Williamson, 1996, p. 5.

[3] Other terms being used are "asset-light lifestyle", "collaborative economy", "peer economy" and "access economy". They can involve C2C, B2C, C2B and B2B "sharing".

[4] Other examples are Cohealo, JustPark, Skillshare, RelayRides and Landshare. The Oxford Dictionary of English defines "sharing economy" as «An economic system in which assets or services are shared between private individuals, either for free or for a fee, typically by means of the Internet». Wosskow (2014) defines "sharing economy" as "online platforms that help people share access to assets, resources, time and skills". This definition underlines an important characteristic of the "sharing economy": the significant level of disintermediation it allows in transactions between providers and final customers.

[5] See P. Guniganti, 2015.

[6] There is a clear difference between, say, Blablacar and Uber. BlaBlaCar connects drivers and passengers willing to travel together between cities and they share the cost of the journey. Uber connects paying customers and taxi-like service providers, who might even work full time in that capacity. However, a distinction between Uber and Airbnb might be more difficult to draw.

[7] According to Sarah Kessler (2015), the real sharing economy (with its vision of "neighborhood sharing", i.e., less consumerism and more sharing) is dead. Many startups that gave real meaning to the concept of "collaborative consumption", a term that was replaced by the term "sharing economy", are now dead or in decline. The better known "brands" such as Uber and Airbnb, are still around in spite of the many difficulties that have faced in several jurisdictions. However, according to some investors and analysts, their headline valuations (US$ 50 for Uber, US$ 24 for Airbnb) are "mere marketing numbers when they reach the harder reality of an IPO" (see Financial Times, November 11th edition, 2015).

[8] When in the presence of goods and services exhibiting non-rivalry but excludability, as is the case in many examples of sharing economies, we are reminded of the so-called "Club Goods Theory". A "Club" is a voluntary group of individuals who derive mutual benefit from sharing one or more of the following: production costs, the members' characteristics, or a good/service characterized by excludable benefits. When production costs are shared and the good is purely private, a "private good club" is being analyzed – see Cornes & Sandler, 1996, p. 347. Of course, in the case of peer-to-peer money lending, 'intertemporal non-rivalry' is absent. But when one talks about "collaborative consumption", one would say some form of non-rivalry has to be present. This characteristic may be less obvious in other types of the "sharing economy".

[9] I am not dealing here with formal 'Licensing Agreements', defined as written agreement entered into by the contractual owner of a property or activity giving permission to another to use that property or engage in an activity in relation to that property, where the property involved can be real, personal or intellectual. Licensing agreements can be an intangible but valuable asset in industries such as technology, biotechnology and publishing. These agreements are a large part of intellectual property law, particularly in terms of enforcement of copyrights, trademarks and patents.

[10] Let us follow De Streel & Larouche (2015) who define disruptive innovation as "a technological innovation that takes place outside the value network of the established firms and introduces a different package of attributes from the one mainstream customers historically value".

[11] By "transaction costs" I mean the costs associated with negotiating, reaching and enforcing agreements. Hence, an easier matching of the right people will typically reduce transaction costs. As mentioned in Williamson (1996), and following K. Arrow's definition of "transaction costs" as 'the costs of running the economic system', if one views

the economic system from the standpoint of contracts, transaction costs can be thought of as the costs of contracting. See also Coase (1988).

[12] See M. Spence, 2015.

[13] See Li Gan & Qi Li (2004) where a matching model is proposed to analyze the efficiency of thin and thick markets.

[14] As an example, this happens when spot labor markets replace long-term employment contracts offered by firms. In the latter case, and contrary to spot labor markets, those firms typically will have to provide benefits to its workers, such as health and disability insurance. Moreover, greater reliance on markets than on firms for the development of economic activities may pose new challenges to competition policy.

[15] As mentioned by L. Einav et al. (2015), eBay may have started as a consumer auction platform but it became a sales channel for many larger (brick-and-mortar) retailers. Labor markets such as oDesk and Freelance have organized firms that bid for jobs, and some peer-to-peer financial service platforms have tried with varying degrees of success to attract professional/dedicated lenders.

[16] See T. Slee, 2013. These reputation systems or schemes used by online platforms may be of their own design and for their own use. But there are also independent quality controllers providing similar services.

[17] See Bolton et al., 2012. The authors analyze reciprocity in feedback giving and the way they may distort the production and content of reputation information in a market, hampering trust and trade efficiency. Guided by feedback patterns observed on eBay and other platforms, they run laboratory experiments to investigate how reciprocity can be managed by changes in the way feedback information flows through the system, leading to more accurate reputation information, more trust, and more efficient trade.

[18] Free online social networks such as Facebook, Twitter, LinkedIn, QZone provide further relevant information about participants' profiles in sharing economies, complementing the information provided by the dedicated internet reputation systems, and increasing the likelihood of achieving a suitable separating equilibrium. Successful participations in the "sharing economy" will foster trust: people's repeated and successful participation in the "sharing economy" enables the accumulation of each participant's "stock of trust" and the overall "stock of trust" of the "sharing economy" itself, as the latter is a function of all the participants' "stocks of trust". Greater trust leads to greater participation in the sharing economy which, in turn, will produce greater trust, provided the number and negative impact of opportunists are kept sufficiently low. "Blockchain" technologies – see *The Economist*, Oct 31st, 2015 – can also be useful in the "sharing economy".

[19] See Wosskov, 2014, and PwC website – interview with Norbert Winkeljohann.

[20] According to a Report from PricewaterhouseCoopers titled "The Sharing Economy" based on a survey of US consumers and published this year, 44% of US consumers are familiar with the sharing economy, 19% of the total US adult population has engaged in a sharing economy transaction, 86% agree it makes life more affordable, 83% agree it makes life more convenient and efficient, 76% agree it is better for the environment, 78% agree it builds a stronger community. Moreover, 7% of the US population are providers in the sharing economy and they cut across age and household income. However, 72% agree they feel that the sharing economy experience is not consistent and 69% agree they will not trust sharing economy companies until they are recommended by someone they trust.

[21] See J. Hall et al. (2015), B. Gurley (2014) and J. Surowiecki (2014).

[22] See the recent work by Ezrachi & Stucke (2015, http://ssrn.com/abstract=2591874) and by Mehra (2015, http://papers.ssrn.com/sol3/papers.cfm?abstract_id=2576341), and the need to revisit the concepts of "agreement" and "intent" for the purpose of antitrust enforcement in an economy where computers and algorithms play an increasing role

in dynamic pricing and market transactions. See also Priluck (2015). On the use online platforms in the "sharing economy" can make of the extensive amounts of data they collect from buyers, sellers and peers in general, and whether there might lead to barriers to entry or foreclosure effects, the reader can be referred to the recent literature on competition issues raised by the so-called "Big Data".

[23] See the April 2015 case on e-commerce dealt with by the US Department of Justice's San Francisco Division, involving David Topkins, the founder of "Poster Revolution", purchased in 2012 by Art.com, concerning an algorithm he apparently had coded that enabled Topkins and his co-conspirators to agree to fix the prices of certain posters sold in the US through Amazon Marketplace – see US District Court, Northern District of California, San Francisco Division, US v. David Topkins, Violation: Title 15, US Code, Section 1 (Price Fixing).

[24] Think of the role played by the price system in a market economy, with prices as conveyors of information on the relative scarcity of the different economic resources. Under a "transaction cost economics" point of view, a similarly important role is played by the information signals sent by thousands of interacting economic agents, in a decentralized fashion, on the trustworthiness and other relevant characteristics of their peers as revealed, if only partially so, by their behavior. The underlying modes of behavior may eventually coalesce into "social norms" or "behavioral standards" and associated expectations, accepted and enforced by a large enough majority of those participating in these online communities, and supported by equally agreed upon "technical standards", even if always evolving and exhibiting different degrees of success.

[25] Still according to PwC Report "The Sharing Economy", 89% agree the sharing economy is based on trust between providers and users, and 64% of consumers say that in the sharing economy, peer regulation is more important than government regulation. These results, together with the arguments developed in this Note, underscore the importance of understanding the sharing economy as "an economy built on trust".

[26] There may be scenarios defined by peer and professional producers/sellers cost functions and by variability in demand that justify the presence of only professional/dedicated producers/sellers in a market equilibrium. In other scenarios, namely when final demand exhibits high variability, both types of producers/sellers may coexist in a market equilibrium – see L. Einav et al. (2015) for an analytical treatment of this issue.

[27] See D. Geradin (2015) for a short but thorough treatment of some of the main challenges posed by Uber to competition policy. See also the March 9th 2013 issue of *The Economist* for an overview of the rise of the "sharing economy". Uber can be regarded as an online two-sided platform where the "Uber pricing algorithm" defines a price structure applied to the taxi-like service provider and the customer, according to which the drivers keep on average 80% of the gross fare.

[28] See the recent Decision by the California Labor Commission, June 2015.

[29] See S. Barrett, 2003. As mentioned by the author, a ministerial proposal to increase the number of taxis by just adding vehicles to existing taxi licenses was challenged in the High Court by hackney drivers of private hire vehicles. This legal challenge was successful and entry to the taxi sector was deregulated by the High Court and not just restricted to those with existing taxi licenses.

References

Barrett, S. (2003): "Regulatory Capture, Property Rights and Taxi Deregulation: A Case Study", *Economic Affairs*, Vol. 23, No. 4, pp. 34-40.

Bolton, Gary et al. (2012): "Engineering Trust: Reciprocity in the Production of Reputation Information", *Management Science*, Vol. 59, No. 2, pp. 265 – 285.

Botsman, Rachel (2013): "The Sharing Economy Lacks a Shared Definition", FastCompany, November 21, 2013.

Botsman, Rachel (2015): "Defining The Sharing Economy: What Is Collaborative Consumption- And What Isn't?" FastCompany, May 27, 2015.

California Labor Commission (2015): Decision for Case No. 11-46739 EK, June 3rd; Barbara Ann Berwick (Plaintiff) vs. Uber Technologies, Inc. and Rasier – CA LLC (Defendants).

Coase, Ronald H. (1988): The Firm, the Market and the Law. Chicago, IL: The University of Chicago Press.

Cornes, Richard & Sandler, Todd (1996) : The Theory of Externalities, Public Goods and Club Goods (2nd edition). Cambridge, England : Cambridge University Press.

De Streel, Alexandre & Larouche, Pierre (2015): "Disruptive Innovation and Competition Policy Enforcement", Note for the 2015 OECD Global Forum on Competition, October 20th.

Einav, Liran et al. (2015): "Peer-To-Peer Markets", NBER Working Paper No. 21496, August.

Ezrachi, Ariel & Stucke, Maurice E. (2015): "Artificial Intelligence & Collusion: When Computers Inhibit Competition", The University of Tennessee College of Law, Legal Studies Research Paper #267, May.

Gan, Li & Li, Qi (2004): "Efficiency of Thin and Thick Markets", NBER Working Paper No. 10815, September.

Geradin, Damien (2015): "Should Uber be allowed to compete in Europe? And if so how?" Competition Policy International, June.

Grossman, Nick (2015): "Regulation, the Internet Way", Harvard University Kennedy School, unpublished paper.

Guniganti, Pallavi (2015): "Driven by Demand", Global Competition Review, February.

Gurley, Bill (2014): "A Deeper Look at Uber's Dynamic Pricing Model", Techmeme, March 11th.

Hall, Jonathan et al. (2015): "The Effects of Uber's Surge pricing: A Case Study", WP, Sept 17th.

Kessler, Sarah (2015): "The 'sharing economy' is dead, and we killed it," FastCompany, September 14th.

Mehar, Salil (2015): "Antitrust and the Robo-Seller: Competition in the Time of Algorithms", Minnesota Law Review, Vol. 100 (Forthcoming).

§ PricewaterhouseCoopers LLP (2015): The Sharing Economy, Report, Consumer Intelligence Series.

Priluck, Jill (2015): "When Bots Collude", The New Yorker magazine, April 25th.

Slee, Tom (2013): "Some Obvious Things about Internet Reputation Systems", Personal Blog.

Spence, Michael (2015): "The Inexorable Logic of the Sharing Economy", Project Syndicate, Sept 28th.

Surowiecki, James (2014): "In Praise of Efficient Price Gouging", MIT Technology Review, August 19th.

Williamson, Oliver (1996): The Mechanisms of Governance. Oxford, England: Oxford University Press.

Wosskow, Debbie (2014): Unlocking the sharing economy: An independent review. Department for Business, Innovation and Skills, UK Government, November.

> "*Uber may become the Myspace or Netscape of ride sharing—that is, a pioneer that could not maintain its market position.*"

The Rise of Uber Comes at a Social Cost

Brishen Rogers

In following excerpted viewpoint, Brishen Rogers argues that there are several concerns about which Uber should be careful as it establishes itself as the groundbreaking company it has come to be known in the ride-sharing space. The author cites specific examples from the recent past to make his points about safety concerns and issues concerning privacy. Brishen Rogers is a professor of law at Temple University's James E. Beardsley School of Law.

As you read, consider the following questions:

1. According to this viewpoint, what are some of the main criticisms Uber has faced thus far?
2. According to the author, what impact do background checks on Uber drivers have on this business?
3. According to the author, about what company policy's details did Minnesota Senator Al Franken write to Uber?

II. Social Costs and Benefits of Uber

Understanding Uber's business model and this transformation allows for a better assessment of the social costs and benefits of Uber's rise. Some such benefits are obvious. Like Airbnb and other sharing-economy firms, Uber may enable far more efficient use of capital and substantially enhance consumer welfare. For example, Uber reduces consumers' incentives to purchase automobiles, almost certainly saving them money and reducing environmental harms.[25] As consumers buy fewer cars, Uber also opens up the remarkable possibility of converting parking spaces to new and environmentally sound uses. Uber may also reduce drunk driving and other accidents. These are all important social goods.

At the same time, Uber has faced criticism along at least six dimensions: First, that it is unfairly competing with taxi drivers by entering their market without following regulations or fare schedules; second, that it aspires to become a monopoly; third, that its cars or drivers are unsafe or underinsured; fourth, that it may invade customers' privacy; fifth, that it enables discrimination by drivers and passengers; and sixth, that it is undermining working standards for taxi drivers and compensating its own drivers poorly.

The first two arguments can be addressed quickly, while the others are more complicated.

Regarding the first, it seems unquestionable that Uber aims to undermine traditional taxi service, and it seems manifestly unfair that taxi drivers and Uber drivers can operate in the same market subject to different rules. This is especially true insofar as Uber floods the market with part-time drivers during peak periods.[26] Uber may therefore cut off one classic path to the American Dream: that taxi drivers can work their way up the income ladder, from a driver to the owner of their own car, and then to an owner of multiple cars. At the same time, to ban Uber on that ground alone may just ratify a regulatory structure that often led to low supply, poor service, and bad pay. The issues discussed below therefore strike me as more important to assessing how Uber and taxis should be allowed to compete.

Regarding the second criticism, it also seems clear that Uber aspires to dominate the ride-sharing sector, and perhaps the car-hire sector more generally. It also wants to become a leading logistics company.[27] Excessive market power in any of these sectors could of course threaten consumer welfare.

Yet it would be a real mistake to regulate Uber out of existence on that basis alone. For one thing, as noted above and explored below, greater horizontal and vertical integration can bring certain public benefits. Moreover, it is not clear that Uber's position at the top of the ride-sharing sector is stable. While Uber's app is revolutionary, it is also easy to replicate. Uber already faces intense competition from Lyft and other ride-sharing companies, competition that should only become more intense given Uber's repeated public relations disasters.[28] While Uber's success relies in part on network effects—more riders and drivers enable a more efficient market—the switching costs for riders and drivers appear to be fairly minimal. Uber may become the Myspace or Netscape of ride sharing—that is, a pioneer that could not maintain its market position. Concerns about monopoly therefore seem premature.[29]

A. Safety

Other concerns are a bit more complicated. For example, courts in Germany and the United States have enjoined some of Uber's services on safety grounds,[30] and not without reason. An Uber driver in San Francisco struck and killed a young girl, possibly at a time when he was distracted by Uber's app. His insurance may not cover her family's losses, and Uber's commercial coverage was not in effect at the time since he was not carrying a fare.[31] Uber drivers have also assaulted passengers and committed other crimes—most notably when a driver in Washington, DC, took several riders on a high-speed chase.[32]

Yet safety will probably not be a major issue in the long run. True, some Uber drivers will assault passengers, and Uber shares causal and moral responsibility for such assaults since it links up drivers and passengers in the first place. This may be an argument for more stringent background checks on drivers, though such checks are no panacea. As the Equal Employment Opportunity Commission (EEOC) has emphasized, background checks have limited predictive value and can have a disparate impact on minority drivers.[33] More generally, however, there is no indication that criminal law will not deter assaults just as well in Uber cars as it does in taxis. In fact, criminal law may work far better, since any passenger who suffers an assault by an Uber driver will actually be able to identify their driver. Not so in a street-hailed cab. Worries about unsafe Uber cars or unsafe driving are of course legitimate, but the experience of riding in a cab in many cities hardly invites confidence that cab drivers or cabs are much better.

Perhaps more importantly, is there any reason to think that problems of dangerous or underinsured Uber drivers will not be self-correcting? Any rash of accidents will lead quickly to public ire and calls for regulation or will create an opening for Uber's competitors. This may of course change if the company fades from public view, as its extremely high media profile is now ensuring that consumers learn of its every misstep. But in the medium term, the company has incentives to insure its drivers, at least while they are carrying Uber passengers. It also has incentives to embrace compromise legislation, such as that recently passed in Washington, DC, that legalizes the service while requiring certain safety inspections, liability insurance levels, and background checks on drivers.[34]

B. Privacy

Uber's use of rider data has also sparked concern, especially after widespread coverage of its possible plan to spy on journalists. The *New York Times* ran a story days after that plan was identified recounting that some users had ceased using the service as a result.[35] One angel investor told the *Times* why she stopped: "I don't want them to have my information, my credit card or my name."[36] Senator Al Franken, of Minnesota, sent a letter to the company requesting information about its privacy practices. "The reports suggest a troubling disregard for customers' privacy," Franken wrote, "including the need to protect their sensitive geolocation data."[37] The fear is obvious, and warranted: Uber's ride data on venture capitalists, journalists, elected officials, and others could be used for all sorts of improper purposes, including corporate espionage and manipulation of regulators. Given the company's take-no-prisoners approach to competitors and critics, this is not far-fetched.

While I am not a privacy expert, I suspect that privacy issues will largely self-correct as well. Unlike Facebook and Google, sale or exploitation of user data does not seem to be a major revenue source for Uber. The aggregate data are what enables Uber to make its market. As a result, if elites such as journalists and venture capitalists cease using Uber out of fear that it will use their data for untoward purposes, the company seems very likely to back down. Failing to do so would create a major opening for other ride-sharing apps with less baggage.

Endnotes

24. See generally Cynthia Estlund, Rebuilding the Law of the Workplace in an Era of Self-Regulation, 105 Colum L Rev 319 (2005); Susan Sturm, Second Generation Employment Discrimination: A Structural Approach, 101 Colum L Rev 458 (2001).

25. Christian Fritz, Mobility-As-a-Service: Turning Transportation into a Software Industry (Venture Beat Dec 13, 2014), online at http://venturebeat.com/2014/12/13/mobility-as-a-service-turning-transportation-into-a-software-industry (visited Feb 26, 2015).

26. Pricing the Surge: The Microeconomics of Uber's Attempt to Revolutionise Taxi Markets (*The Economist* Mar 29, 2014), online at http://www.economist.com/news/finance-and-economics/21599766-microeconomics-ubers-attempt-revolutionise-taxi-markets-pricing-surge (visited Feb 26, 2015).

27. See Emily Badger, Why Uber Is Joining the Race to Dominate Urban Logistics, Wash Post Wonkblog (Wash Post Apr 8, 2014), online at http://www.washingtonpost.com/blogs/wonkblog/wp/2014/04/08/why-uber-is-joining-the-race-to-dominate-logistics (visited Feb 26, 2015).

28. See Ben Smith, Uber Executive Suggests Digging Up Dirt on Journalists (Buzzfeed Nov 17, 2014), online at http://www.buzzfeed.com/bensmith/uber-executive-suggests-digging-up-dirt (visited Feb 26, 2015); Sarah Lacy, The Horrific Trickle-Down of Asshole Culture: Why I've Just Deleted Uber from My Phone (PandoDaily Oct 22, 2014), online at http://pando.com/2014/10/22/the-horrific-trickle-down-of-asshole-culture... (visited Feb 26, 2015) (describing recent company acts as demonstrating "sexism and misogyny").

29. The related issue of Uber's "surge pricing," under which it raises rates at times of very high demand, is troubling but should also be self-correcting. If riders are sufficiently upset

about that pricing, the bad press and loss of goodwill should drive riders toward other companies.

30. See Karin Matussek, Uber Must Stop Car Service in Germany's Two Largest Cities (Bloomberg Sept 26, 2014), online at http://www.bloomberg.com/news/2014-09 -26/uber-faces-ban-in-berlin-after-overturning-german-wide-measure.html (visited Feb 26, 2015) (quoting the spokesman for a Berlin court, who claimed that the injunction was "necessary to protect customers from dangers to life and limb"). See also Luz Lazo, Virginia Reaches Deal with Uber, Lyft, to Allow Services to Operate in the State, Wash Post Dr. Gridlock Blog (*Wash Post* Aug 6, 2014), online at http://www.washingtonpost .com/ blogs/dr-gridlock/wp/2014/08/06/virginia-reaches-deal-with-uber-lyft-to-allow -services-to-operate-in-the-state (visited Feb 26, 2015) (noting that Virginia officials lifted a cease-and-desist order against Uber only once the company reached a settlement with the state that ensured consumer safety and a level playing field for transportation providers).

31. See Kale Williams and Kurtis Alexander, Uber Sued over Girl's Death in S.F., SFGate (*San Francisco Chronicle* Jan 28, 2014), online at http://www.sfgate.com/bayarea/article /Uber-sued-over-girl-s-death-in-S-F-5178921.php (visited Feb 26, 2015).

32. See Julie Zauzmer and Lori Aratani, Man Visiting D.C. Says Uber Driver Took Him on a Wild Ride, Wash Post Dr. Gridlock Blog (*Wash Post* July 9, 2014), online at http://www .washingtonpost.com/blogs/dr-gridlock/wp/2014/07/09/man-visiting-d-c-says-uber -driver-took-him-on-wild-ride (visited Feb 26, 2015).

33. See Equal Employment Opportunity Commission, Consideration of Arrest and Conviction Records in Employment Decisions under Title VII of the Civil Rights Act of 1964 *11 (Guidance No 915-002, Apr 25, 2012), online at http://www.eeoc.gov /laws/ guidance/upload/arrest_conviction.pdf (visited Feb 26, 2015) (suggesting that employers may avoid disparate impact liability upon a showing that a policy adequately accounted for "the nature and gravity of the offense or conduct," "the time that has passed since the offense or conduct," and "the nature of the job held or sought"). Under those policies, an absolute ban on contracting with drivers with criminal convictions would be discriminatory, though of course Uber is not subject to Title VII because it does not employ drivers. See El v Southeastern Pennsylvania Transportation Authority, 479 F3d 232, 248 (3d Cir 2007) (upholding summary judgment for the defendant, which terminated the plaintiff in accordance with a policy of screening for past criminal convictions, but noting the "reasonable inference that [the defendant] has no real basis for asserting that its policy accurately distinguishes between applicants that do and do not present an unacceptable level of risk").

34. See Martin Di Caro, Ridesharing Legislation Passes D.C. Council over Protests of Cabbies, Teamsters (WAMU Oct 29, 2014) online at http://wamu.org/news/14/10/28 / uberx_lyft_win_key_battle_in_dc_council (visited Feb 26, 2015). But see Marc Lifsher, Ride-Sharing Firms Shift into Overdrive to Kill Insurance Bill (*LA Times* Aug 24, 2014), online at http://www.latimes.com/business/la-fi-capitol-business-beat-20140825-story .html (visited Feb 26, 2015) (noting Uber's strong opposition to California legislation backed by the insurance and taxi industries).

35. Laura M. Holson, To Delete or Not to Delete: That's the Uber Question (*NY Times* 36. Id.

37. Mike Isaac, Uber's Privacy Practices Questioned by Senator Franken, *NY Times* Bits Blog (*NY Times* Nov 19, 2014), online at http://bits.blogs.nytimes.com/2014/11/19/ senator-questions-uber-on-privacy-practices (visited Feb 26, 2015).

> *"As we have seen, in some cases, like Rent the Runway, business model choices may evolve over time in response to user experiences, profitability expectations, societal impacts, or investor preferences."*

The Sharing Economy Has Many Business Models

Boyd Cohen

In the following viewpoint, Dr. Boyd Cohen, along with his colleague, Pablo Muñoz, explore the complexities of the sharing economy. They looked at hundreds of sources, which used thirty-six sharing business startups. They assessed the data under the umbrella of six main categories, which they identified, and which are laid out in the article. Ultimately, they encourage local and regional governments to consider all facets of the sharing economy as they develop regulations. Cohen is the co-author of Climate Capitalism: Capitalism in the Age of Climate Change *and Director of Innovation and Professor of Entrepreneurship, Sustainability and Smart Cities at the Universidad del Desarrollo in Santiago, Chile.*

"Making Sense of the Many Business Models in the Sharing Economy," by Boyd Cohen, Mansueto Ventures LLC, June 4, 2016. Reprinted by permission.

As you read, consider the following questions:

1. In this viewpoint, what "style" tool did the researchers come up with that includes transaction, business approach, governance model, platform type, technology, and shared resources?
2. According to this viewpoint, what conventional company, known for car rentals, purchased Zipcar for $500 million?
3. According to this viewpoint, in what direction do the author and his research colleague see the collaborative business model going, over time?

Is Uber even part of the sharing economy? Does Airbnb's business model have a positive or negative impact on communities? Are on-demand startups like TaskRabbit leveraging exploitative business models? What is the right approach for local governments when it comes to regulating the sharing economy?

These are just a few of the persistent questions regarding the new range of businesses reshaping our business landscape. Some prefer to see the world as black and white: "Sharing will save the world by reducing our environmental consumption while solving income inequality" versus "sharing platforms are really just a share-washing platform version of capitalism for the 1%." But in reality, the emerging sharing landscape is very complex.

To begin to get under the hood of the business models of sharing-economy players, my colleague, Pablo Muñoz and I analyzed hundreds of sources of data on 36 different sharing business startups representative of Jeremiah Owyang's Honeycomb model, a graphical depiction of the different sectors where sharing startups have gained traction. While the Honeycomb model has been of great use in framing the diversity of sectors being impacted or disrupted by the sharing economy, it does not provide any insights on the underlying business models across the 12 different sharing-economy sectors that Owyang identifies. So we identified six key dimensions of sharing-economy business models, each of them with three distinct decisions that can be made by sharing startups. We converted this into what we hope is a useful tool, the Sharing Business Model Compass.

Four of these dimensions—transaction, business approach, governance model and platform type—offer business model decision choices roughly on a continuum from more market-based sharing (i.e. platform capitalism) towards commons-based sharing (i.e. platform cooperatives). While the other two dimensions—technology and shared resources—have decisions relatively agnostic to market or commons orientations.

If you're thinking of starting a sharing-based business, we believe this tool is useful in demonstrating that there are a plethora of key decisions unique to the sharing economy that entrepreneurs must make along the way. If you're thinking about the sharing economy in general—and how it interacts with people, government, and the world—this framework can be helpful in explaining what specific parts of the sharing economy you find optimal—or objectionable.

Technology

Within this dimension, there are three choices: tech-driven, tech-enabled, and low/no-tech. Tech-driven business models are ones leverage technology not just to connect users but also to complete the transaction without the need for offline interaction. Crowdfunding sites like Kickstarter and Indiegogo and online learning portals such as Udacity and Coursera fall in the tech-driven category. The majority of the startups we studied fall more in the tech-enabled category, which represents business models reliant on technology to facilitate the connections but require or are enhanced by offline interactions. Uber would fall into this category, as would Wallapop, a fast-growing hyper-local mobile classified business for P2P reselling of used goods. While most of what we think about in the sharing-economy space is at least enabled by technology, there are still many startups in the sharing space where technology is at most a supporting-tool but not critical (i.e. low/

no-tech). Co-working spaces and shared commercial kitchens are good examples of the low/no-tech business model, while other models such as the Repair Café are hyper-local, nonprofit, no-tech sharing actors.

Transaction

We observed three variations in transaction types: market, alternative, and free. Perhaps the most extreme version of market transaction is Uber, which does not only vary pricing based on demand, but also includes the highly controversial surge pricing. Most of the scaled, venture capital-backed sharing startups—such as Airbnb and Rent the Runway—opt for market pricing. The alternative option is jut starting to emerge. While there are perhaps fewer scaled examples so far, Bliive, a rapidly globalizing time bank out of Brazil is a good example. Instead of on-demand models that seek to facilitate economic transactions between a service provider and a home-owner, time banks allow service providers to earn "time dollars" to be exchanged later for other service provided at a later date from someone else in the community. Yerdle, a P2P service for exchanging used goods also falls into the alternative category. Instead of exchange for cash, users earn Yerdle dollars for acquiring other goods in the future. Peerby, another P2P used goods exchange, founded in Amsterdam in 2011, offers a completely free service. Of course, many bike-share services are free or just require an annual deposit. While you may think that free bike-sharing services have no business model, and perhaps are just subsidized public transit options, think again. Most of the scaled bike-sharing services in cities like Paris, Mexico City, London, and New York City, generate most of their revenue through sponsorships or advertising models.

Business Approach

There are three primary options from sharing providers with respect to the business approach: profit-driven, hybrid, and mission-driven. We consider Uber, Upwork and eBay to be amongst the many sharing platforms that are profit-driven. Profit does not have to be a bad word, however, and we do not believe a sharing firm that is profit-driven to necessarily be bad corporate citizens. But there are viable alternatives. Hybrid models are those that are usually founded as for-profits but have a clearly stated goal that drives them to create social and/or environmental benefits in communities. Zipcar, sold to Avis for $500 million is a good example as it was founded, and stayed true to the goal of reducing congestion and contamination in cities, while providing access to a vehicle for people who could not afford, or choose not to own one (or a second) vehicle. Kickstarter, at a minimum would also be considered a hybrid approach as they aspire to support creative projects around the globe and to be good corporate citizens. At the end of 2014, Kickstarter joined the growing group of responsible companies who became a certified B-Corporation, which obligates them to transparently track and monitor their sustainability performance. Kiva is even further down the path of a mission-driven company, having formed as "a nonprofit organization with a mission to connect people through lending to alleviate poverty." Certainly the more than 1,000 Repair Cafes around the globe would fit squarely in the mission-driven category as well.

Shared Resources

In her book, Peers, Inc., Robin Chase (the founder of Zipcar) suggested that sharing business models optimize under-utilized resources in society. We agree, although as we studied the business models we realized that there are really three ways sharing startups seek to achieve this. They either optimize new resources, help find a new home for used resources, or leverage facilitate the optimization of under-utilized, existing resources. Zipcar itself is a good example of the optimization of new resources as more often than not their fleet is made up entirely of newly acquired vehicles. Rent the Runway actually started with a model focused on the optimization of under-utilized existing resources (e.g. dresses worn once to a wedding), but have shifted their model in recent years

REGULATION

Generally, "regulation" refers to the use of legal instruments to implement social and economic policy objectives. Judge Richard Posner defines economic regulation as follows: "Properly defined, the term refers to taxes and subsidies of all sorts as well as to explicit legislative and administrative controls over rates, entry, and other facets of economic activity." When market practices lead to inefficient or inequitable outcomes (a situation often referred to as a "market failure")—for example, due to asymmetric information, the problem of public goods, the threat of monopoly, or the existence of externalities that are not naturally internalized by market participants—regulation may be supplied as a corrective measure. In the absence of technological, self-regulatory, or governmental intervention, peer-to-peer exchange is susceptible to a variety of forms of market failure.

"Self-Regulation and Innovation in the Peer-to-Peer Sharing Economy," by Molly Cohen and Arun Sundararajan, 2015.

to the optimization of new resources where the company acquires new clothing for rental to users of their platform. Many of the P2P models for used items we already mentioned (e.g. Wallapop, eBay, Peerby), fall into the "new home for used resource" category. In the optimization of under-utilized resources category, P2P car-sharing and carpooling models like Blablacar fit well. Similarly, crowd-shipping models such as Shipizy also belong here.

Governance Model

The governance models for sharing startups range significantly, from traditional corporate structures to collaborative governance models to cooperative models. Corporate structures seem to be the choice, not surprisingly so, for most venture capital-backed business models in the sharing economy (e.g. Uber, Airbnb, Upwork, Rent the Runway). Yet some scaled sharing businesses such as Kiva embrace collaborative approaches to working with users and other stakeholders in sourcing, implementing, and monitoring projects funded through the platform.

While we found a relatively small amount of projects currently embracing collaborative business models, we expect this number will grow significantly over time, as the benefits to more engagement with users on the platform become more apparent. The cooperative governance model for sharing-economy startups, though, has yet to get much traction—although some of the components of cooperative models can be seen in alternative and cryptocurrency startups. Also, there are reports of taxi drivers in cities joining forces to form cooperatives in an attempt to respond to Uber competition. There is a big drive from within the sharing community to support more "platform cooperatives" as evidenced by the Platform Cooperativism event (and the numerous conversations and smaller-scale events since) which was highly attended in New York City at the end of 2015.

Platform Type

While we are used to thinking of the sharing economy as being peer-to-peer (P2P), in reality, there are at least three common platforms in use: B2B, business to crowd and P2P. In the B2B category you can find companies like Yardclub, founded by Caterpillar, which facilitates the rental of Caterpillar tractors for construction sites. Similarly, Cohealo facilitates the sharing of expensive hospital equipment between hospitals. In the Business to Crowd category, companies like Zipcar and Rent the Runway choose to own the resources that will be exchanged within the user community. And platforms where peers exchange products or services with each other, and where the platform provider owns virtually none of the shared assets (such as Airbnb, Task Rabbit, Indiegogo, Blablacar, etc.) fall into the classical P2P category.

Implications

As we have seen, in some cases, like Rent the Runway, business model choices may evolve over time in response to user experiences, profitability expectations, societal impacts, or investor preferences. Importantly, the compass demonstrates there is a lot of grey in sharing business models. In fact, if one assumes that all sharing business models contain the six dimensions addressed in the Compass, and that all sharing startups must choose just one option within each dimension, this leads to a total possible of 729 unique business models. That is to say, there is a lot of diversity within the sharing business and this diversity has potentially significant implications for the scalability, profitability, investability, and the social and environmental impact of users and communities as a whole.

We believe that sharing startup founding teams would be wise to discuss these decisions early in the formation of the venture.

We also believe that local and regional governments seeking to regulate the sharing economy would be wise to think through the underlying dimensions of different business models in order to develop more sound policy to encourage the type of sharing business models desired while disincentivizing or regulating elements that are least desired.

> "*How do the new wave of internet businesses fit into regulatory structures that were designed for a bricks-and-mortar world? Badly!*"

The Traditional Economy Can Thrive from Competition from the Sharing Economy

Stephen King

In the following viewpoint, Stephen King argues that the new generation of businesses built on internet-based technology don't have a clear position in the traditionally brick-and-mortar-driven economy and that a smoother way of presenting both to consumers needs to exist. He asks the reader how to protect consumer interests, how to avoid vested interests using regulation to stop entry and competition, and how to prepare for future issues regarding competition. King is a professor of economics at Monash University in Melbourne, Australia. His areas of expertise include trade practice economics, regulation, and industrial organization.

"The Three Regulatory Challenges for the Sharing Economy," by Stephen King, *The Conversation*, February 19, 2015. http://theconversation.com/the-three-regulatory -challenges-for-the-sharing-economy-37808. CC BY ND 4.0 International.

As you read, consider the following questions:

1. According to this viewpoint, what are a few ways consumers can be protected as the sharing economy grows?
2. According to the author, what is one of the most important elements of competition?
3. According to this viewpoint, what is a key result of the growth of new businesses built on the growth of internet-based technology, for consumers?

New internet businesses are transforming dusty old industries. The current wave includes Uber (hire cars), Airbnb (accommodation) and Freelancer (labour services).

But there have been plenty of others over the past twenty years. Email has bankrupted postal services. Skype put a rocket under telephone companies. Google has transformed information and advertising.

There will be plenty more in the near future.

How do the new wave of internet businesses fit into regulatory structures that were designed for a bricks-and-mortar world?

Badly!

The Productivity Commission is currently investigating the barriers facing new businesses. It is taking particular interest in digital start-ups. However, the problems go much deeper.

There are three regulatory challenges for Australia when dealing with internet businesses in the sharing economy:

1. How do we protect consumer interests?
2. How do we avoid vested interests using regulation to stop entry and competition?
3. How do we prepare for future competition issues?

Consumer protection

Your Uber car is involved in an accident. The driver has standard insurance, not commercial insurance. So any property loss is not covered.

You rent an Airbnb apartment only to find out that the apartment has been sublet in violation of the lease. You are evicted.

You lease out your apartment on Airbnb. A few days later the police call. The apartment has just been raided. The tenants were using it as a pop-up brothel.

Commercial arrangements can go wrong for any business. Internet businesses are neither more nor less likely to raise problems. However, from the consumers' perspective, these businesses operate outside normal guidelines because they claim to be matching platforms, not direct service providers.

Uber doesn't employ its drivers. It checks them and uses a ratings system to maintain standards, but it would claim that it is not formally liable for poor driver conduct. Similarly, Airbnb states that local laws are the local service provider's problem.

Is this legal and is it good enough?

The Courts will check the legality. But relevant precedent is probably years away. Further, Court decisions may be inconsistent between jurisdictions. In Australia, the High Court ruled that Google is simply a publisher and not liable for third-party advertising content. However, the European 'right to be forgotten' laws make Google liable for third party web-pages that can be accessed through its search engine.

The platforms may ask us to trust them. After all, their reputation depends on the quality of the services provided through their platforms. But this is not good enough. Relying on the market and reputation to sort out consumer protection issues can lead to lots of damage on the way. And despite the best efforts of a platform, bad operators will get onto the system.

Light-handed accreditation regulation will also be imperfect, but it can help the internet platforms work better for consumers.

So Uber drivers may need to be accredited, to ensure they have safe cars and appropriate insurance. Tripadvisor reviews will need to be presented with appropriate caveats. Airbnb apartments should not be advertised in a way that is misleading and deceptive. And the platforms cannot simply shrug their shoulders and say, "not our problem". The platform will have some responsibility to check that their suppliers meet appropriate legal standards.

The platforms themselves should recognise this, which perhaps explains Uber's recent change of heart. The alternative is either to operate outside the law and be sued to death, or to watch a new regulatory bureaucracy grow around their business. Cooperation and compliance, death by lawsuit or strangulation by red tape. They are the options facing the internet businesses.

Vested interest regulation

No business likes competition. Existing bricks and mortar businesses will not simply yield to more efficient internet-based businesses. They will put up a fight and part of the fight will be to try and use regulation to strangle the new businesses.

Of course, incumbents will not put it that way. The official line will be about protecting consumers. So when taxi license owners protest against Uber or hotel chains complain about Airbnb, the language is about consumer interest, not profit protection.

But it is competition that delivers value for consumers. Governments need to separate out self-interested claims by incumbents from real consumer concerns.

This is not easy. Vested interests will blow out of proportion any incident involving the internet entrant while ignoring similar incidents that have occurred through their own service.

Governments need to have the courage and insight to recognise incumbent rent seeking and to hold out against it. That can be difficult. The bricks-and-mortar businesses fighting against the entrants may be large (think Harvey Norman and the internet tax debate), and will have a lot at stake.

But as Andrew Leigh has noted:

> "[F]orward-thinking regulators are increasingly realising that the sharing economy can deliver big benefits for consumers. ... the benefits are real and the risks are manageable."

Competition rules

In technology, today's small entrants are tomorrow's dominant firms. Shareholders in Uber, Airbnb, Tripadvisor, Freelancer, and so on are investing their money in the hope of a profit. And if they succeed by helping consumers, then that is fantastic. However, as these businesses grow, they may be tempted to make easy money through market power rather than competition.

For example, Uber currently does not require that drivers are exclusive. As David Plouffe of Uber noted at a recent Grattan Institute event, a driver can drive for Uber, Lyft, or anyone else. But will these rules continue to hold if Uber (or someone else) grows to dominate the ride sharing market?

These concerns are not hypothetical. We have seen large businesses use various tactics, including exclusivity arrangements, to make new entry hard. In supermarkets, Aldi had a hard time expanding in Australia due to exclusivity arrangements between the major chains and the shopping centres. These were eliminated after the ACCC's 2008 grocery inquiry. Since then, Aldi has rapidly expanded.

Internet based businesses that grow dominant may try similar tactics.

This means that competition regulators will need to be watchful. In particular, the terms and conditions used in contracts between platforms and both suppliers and buyers need careful scrutiny. If they involve exclusivity arrangements or 'reference competitors' say through 'most favoured customer' pricing, then the alarm bells should start ringing.

Two caveats.

First, these concerns hold for all large businesses, not just those on the internet.

Second, in fast changing areas of technology, attempts by incumbents to hold out entry are often doomed to failure. As historic antitrust cases against IBM and Microsoft in the US illustrate, the market will often act faster than regulators and the courts.

Bring internet businesses inside the regulatory tent

New businesses built on internet-based technologies have, are and will continue to transform many industries. The result is better services at cheaper prices for all Australians.

But these businesses cannot and do not live in a regulatory vacuum. They cannot grow as regulatory cowboys. But, vested interests will be more than happy to strangle them with red tape. Getting the balance right will be difficult for both government and regulators. But if we get it right, the potential gains are huge.

> *"New platforms are creating new stakeholders in need of protection, and those same platforms are transforming previously effective self-regulatory systems into barriers to innovation."*

Regulations for Traditional Businesses Will Not Work for Businesses in the Sharing Economy

Urs Gasser

In the following viewpoint, Urs Gasser points out what he refers to as misalignments, meaning challenges or disconnects, between the business regulations currently in place and their hold on the businesses in the sharing economy. These regulations were created at a time when more conventional businesses were the only option available, and with the onset of the sharing economy, a clear need for a shift and an introduction of new regulations has become apparent. Gasser is executive director for the Berkman Center for Internet & Society at Harvard University and Professor of Practice at Harvard Law School.

"The Sharing Economy: Disruptive Effects on Regulation and Paths Forward," by Urs Gasser, Swiss Re, June 6, 2016. Reprinted by permission.

As you read, consider the following questions:

1. According to this viewpoint, how does the sharing economy affect traditional regulations?
2. According to the author, how have professional organizations historically contributed to regulating business practices?
3. According to this viewpoint, what are a few key tools that can be used for regulating the sharing economy?

Just as the sharing economy is disrupting many traditional economic models and relationships, it is also creating misalignments between existing regulations and the harms they are meant to prevent.

The same forces that are upending business models are creating challenges for regulators around the globe. Increasingly, the laws written to regulate taxicabs, hotels, and other industries fit poorly with the new platforms, providers, and consumers using the sharing economy. Regulators must adapt and address these misalignments by viewing regulation not as a binary choice between more or less intervention, but as a range of regulatory tools that need be carefully adjusted to fit the diverse ecosystem of new business models, producers, and platforms.

1. New Innovations and New Stakeholders

One of the most powerful elements of the sharing economy is how it has enabled innovative services that simply would not have been possible without the emergence of new platforms connecting potential consumers with under-utilised property or skills. In the absence of a platform such as Uber or Lyft, it would be difficult to make an income roaming the streets in an unmarked car hoping to find strangers in need of a ride.

Moreover, as more people all over the world increasingly become comfortable arranging and paying for services online, it has made it feasible to offer highly specialised, niche services that might not scale in traditional markets. In Jakarta, Indonesia, which has one of lowest rates of taxis per person in Asia, the sharing economy enables a company like Ojek Syari to connect female drivers with Muslim women who are uncomfortable with male drivers. This ability to bring together people who might otherwise not be consumers with people who might otherwise not be producers is both a strength of the sharing economy but also a source of regulatory challenges.

Traditional regulations often assume a particular set of producers and a particular set of consumers. The sharing economy, however, is upending those assumptions and creating a misalignment in regulation. New platforms are creating new stakeholders in need of protection, and those same platforms are transforming previously effective self-regulatory systems into barriers to innovation. In both cases, these misalignments need to be addressed.

2. New Stakeholders in Need of Protection, New Problems in Need of Remediation

Traditional regulations are designed to protect certain vulnerable relationships or address particular problems that emerge from those relationships. For example, non-discrimination and common carrier regulations for hotels are designed to protect travelers or others whose need for accommodations and lack of negotiation leverage makes them particularly vulnerable to predatory practices. These traditional regulations often protect weaker consumers against large, professional, business savvy service providers.

In the sharing economy, however, both the consumer and the provider may be in need of regulatory protection. What protections keep Uber drivers safe from abusive riders? What protections help a homeowner after an Airbnb guest destroys their property? Non-professional service providers can be just as vulnerable to harm as consumers, but traditional regulation overlooks these new market participants, creating a misalignment that leaves many stakeholders vulnerable.

Additionally, the sharing economy is creating negative externalities that traditional regulation is often ill-equipped to address. For example, ride sharing can lead to increased road noise, pollution, and traffic. And short-term rentals, like Airbnb, can lead to increased noise and foot traffic in apartment buildings or quiet neighborhoods. Regulations like zoning laws are effective at keeping big hotels out of residential neighborhoods, but they frequently have little to say about renting out an apartment or house for a week or two. Some cities have tried to reduce these negative externalities by tweaking existing regulations. San Francisco, for instance, has limited the number of days a dwelling can be rented. But these approaches can be overly restrictive, creating a misalignment.

3. Old Models of Self-Regulation as a Barrier to Innovation

Before the sharing economy, traditional regulation often operated hand-in-hand with professional organisations and guilds that would self-police their industries to ensure quality services. Depending on the industry, professional organisations might establish standards, ethics, and licensing requirements, administer licensing exams, collect fees, or even take punitive actions against bad actors. The sharing economy does not fit neatly into this traditional model, creating a misalignment of regulation. In response to lower-cost competition from the sharing economy, these professional organisations have often created barriers to innovation, encouraging stricter regulations or outright bans.

The battle between the taxicab industries and ride-sharing platforms highlights this misalignment. Typically, taxi quality was controlled through cooperation between governments and large taxi fleet companies. Governments could limit competition through exclusive medallions, administer licensing exams for drivers, and set insurance requirements and other standards; fleet operators could ensure vehicles were safe and could identify and discipline dangerous drivers. Ride-sharing threatens this balance. As long as they exist outside of traditional taxi regulations, ride-sharing drivers do not buy expensive medallions, take special licensing exams, or carry expensive commercial insurance, enabling them to offer services at lower costs.

This misalignment has often provoked the taxicab industry to push for stricter regulation of ride-sharing. In the US, multiple cities including Miami, Houston, Portland, Austin, and New Orleans have outright banned services like Uber. Other cities, such as Minneapolis and Detroit, have subjected ride-sharing services to taxicab regulations. In the EU, Belgium and Germany have banned ride-sharing services, with a German court calling it unfair competition for local taxis. And in Singapore, the Transport Minister recently initiated a review of ride-sharing services out of concern that the government may need to "level the playing field" to protect traditional taxi drivers[1]. Not everyone agrees that the proper response to the misalignment is stricter regulation. Neelie Kroes, Former EU Commission Vice President for Digital Agenda, argued that the Belgian ban on ride-sharing served to protect the "taxi cartel" and stifle innovation[3].

Addressing these misalignments is critical. Effective regulations should keep both consumers and producers safe. And effective regulations should reduce negative externalities without suppressing productive innovation. Given these competing tensions, where do policymakers begin in realigning outdated regulatory systems?

4. Realigning Regulation Through An Array of Regulatory Tools

Although the sharing economy contributes to a misalignment between markets and regulation, it simultaneously provides policymakers with more flexible tools for more effective regulation. Governments that are able to adopt these flexible approaches to regulation will be best positioned to take advantage of the opportunities of the sharing economy. These flexible approaches include: (1) enabling new forms of self regulation; (2) creating flexible regulations; and (3) investing in innovation.

A. New Technological and Platform Approaches to Self Regulation

Self regulation has long been a core element of traditional markets and services. For example, in order to protect investors and securities trading, the US financial industry, with approval from the US Congress, regulates itself through the Financial Industry Regulatory Authority (FINRA). And as described above, taxi commissions frequently rely on taxi companies to maintain fleets and regulate driver behaviour. But as the sharing economy has disrupted traditional self-regulatory models, it has created opportunities for new self-regulatory approaches that rely on new technology and new platforms.

Self regulation is most effective when it places responsibility with the entities that have the best incentives to regulate, have the greatest pool of information from which to identify negative actors or behaviour, and are best positioned to take corrective action. In many cases, sharing economy platforms have the right incentives, an incredible amount of information, and are best able to control those consuming and providing services through their platforms. For that reason, new technological and reputation-based mechanisms of self regulation can be a key tool for regulating the sharing economy.

- *Incentives*: Sharing economy platforms rely on user trust. Consumers will not return to platforms if they have a bad experience. If a short-term rental is in much worse condition than how it appeared on the rental platform, consumers will feel cheated and deceived. Even more seriously, high publicity cases like the Uber driver convicted of rape in Delhi, India in 2015 have not only generated bad publicity for the platform, but have also catalysed government opposition to the services. For that reason, sharing economy platforms are often highly incentivised to regulate the quality of services on their platform.
- *Information*: Sharing economy platforms can tap into significant pools of data in order to improve their self

regulation. Platforms can use reputation systems, user ratings, social network analysis, and a variety of other analytical tools to collect and assess information about the consumers and providers on the platform. For example, Airbnb's "Verified ID" system, asks some users to provide photos of government identification or links to other social network platforms. Although this data collection can sometimes be intrusive, it can also empower platforms, producers, and consumers to make more informed decisions in a powerful feedback loop. Consumers can choose highly rated producers, just as producers can choose not to work for poorly rated consumers. And platforms can continue to improve the quality and fairness of the data they collect and their ratings methodologies.

- *Ability to Act*: Platforms are in a powerful position to take action. Not only can they remove access from poorly behaving actors, but they can also regulate each transaction. For that reason, platforms are in a better position to regulate tax payments and monitor compliance with local laws than government agencies. The platforms can also offer economies of scale and centralisation that can help their non-professional consumers and producers who might otherwise struggle to understand when to collect taxes or how to get commercial insurance. In fact, all of these factors can work in concert; Airbnb, for example, shares with insurance companies de-identified data about its hosts in order to provide them with insurance.

There is tremendous opportunity for self-regulation in the sharing economy, but it is by no means an exhaustive regulatory solution. First, the incentives to self regulate do not fall equally across all stakeholders. For example, a ride-sharing platform may have less incentive to ensure fair wages or reasonable hours for drivers, particularly if there is a surplus of potential drivers. Similarly, absent external regulation, platforms may lack the incentives to provide less profitable services, such as handicapped accessible services or services in low-income neighborhoods. Second, the technological tools of reputation systems may reinforce existing biases. A reputation system that looks at the strength of social network connections, for instance, may be biased toward those with higher incomes and larger networks.

B. Adapting Regulations for Greater Transparency and Broader Protections

Given that self regulation is not a complete solution to these regulatory misalignments, there remains a need for flexible regulations that address the gaps where self-regulation is insufficient. Often, these new regulations focus on improving transparency or adapting existing regulations in ways that are more inclusive of the new participants in the sharing economy.

- Transparency: Improving transparency in the sharing economy can help all participants make better and more efficient decisions. For example, 2014 regulations in Amsterdam require short-term rental platforms to work with hosts to prominently display relevant laws and regulations around the rental property. Similarly, a 2016 regulation in London requires ride-sharing platforms to provide fare estimates before the ride begins.

- Inclusiveness: Expanding the inclusiveness of regulations can help remove ambiguity from existing regulations that do not clearly apply to the new kinds of participants in the sharing economy. For example, Amsterdam and San Francisco have recently clarified that short-term rental platforms are responsible for collecting and remitting local taxes on behalf of hosts. Similarly, London recently required that ride-sharing platforms provide live customer support for fielding consumer complaints. These regulations place obligations on some of the new participants in the sharing economy (particularly the platforms) that existing regulations did not contemplate.

These forms of regulation demonstrate an approach that is more nuanced than simply leaving the sharing economy unregulated, regulating the sharing economy under existing regulations, or banning it outright. In fact, in several of these cases, the regulations were developed with the input and collaboration of various stakeholders, including the platforms themselves.

C. Supporting the Sharing Economy Through Regulation

Some jurisdictions have begun to recognise that not only can flexible regulation of the sharing economy help contain its more harmful aspects, but it can also become an advantage. These policymakers have realised that the decisions that they make with respect to regulating the sharing economy will in turn impact the extent to which their region benefits from the innovation and positive impacts of these new markets.

In many respects, the approach that policymakers take with respect to the sharing economy is tied to their approach to supporting technology and innovation more broadly. After Belgium banned Uber, Vice President Kroes stated that the ban "sends a bad anti-tech message about Brussels, which is already in the 4G dark ages[3]." Policymakers and regions that are viewed as hostile to technology, innovation, and the sharing economy may find it harder to attract startups and benefit from innovative new services.

By contrast, some policymakers are actively using regulation as a tool to attract innovative new businesses. For example, the Seoul city government recently announced plans to spend USD 240000 supporting and promoting sharing economy startups. It can be difficult to prevent harm while also creating a regulatory environment that does not punish innovative companies that do not fit neatly into existing regulations. However, some policymakers are working to find the right balance and are even investing public money into supporting the growth of those innovative companies.

5. Rewarding Regulatory Flexibility

Innovative sharing economy businesses often operate in spaces that do not clearly fit into existing regulatory categories. This poses a challenge for regulators. Leaving these new markets unregulated is usually not an option; it is important to make sure that vulnerable consumers and producers are protected and that negative externalities are reduced. Additionally, regulation can be important to ensure that access to the benefits of the sharing economy is not limited to certain geographic regions, incomes, physical abilities, or other characteristics. The difficulty is in providing these protections in a way that does not stifle innovative new technologies and services.

Legal scholar Orly Lobel has observed that "policymakers have been experimenting with more participatory and collaborative models of regulation, in which government, industry, and society share responsibility for achieving policy goals. Under this model, platform companies can be viewed as partners, rather than adversaries, of the legal process[4]." Policymakers who can offer more flexible regulatory approaches will be most likely to address the misalignments in regulation while simultaneously encouraging the growth of sharing economies. This may involve embracing self regulation where it makes sense and where it takes advantage of technological advantages inherent in new platforms. And where self regulation is insufficient, it may involve flexible new regulations that boost transparency and ensure vulnerable producers and consumers are protected. In many cases, these regulations can be developed in cooperation and with input from a variety of stakeholders.

Across the US, Europe, and Asia, the kinds of markets most impacted by the sharing economy are those with a history of significant top-down regulation: transportation, lodging, employment, and others. Because of that, at this early moment in the history of the sharing economy, the challenges and misalignments in each region are relatively similar when viewed from a bird's eye perspective. However, as the sharing economy grows, regulators that can move beyond command and control regulatory systems and can orchestrate the wide range of regulatory tools available will be best able to deliver on the benefits of the sharing economy while avoiding its pitfalls.

Endnotes

1. Eileen Yu, "Singapore review of ride-sharing economy should be about protecting consumers, not taxi operators," ZDNet, Oct. 21, 2015, http://www.zdnet.com/article/singapore-review-of-ride-sharing-economy-should-be-about-protecting-consumers-not-taxi-operators/.
2. Nick Summers, "EU Commission VP Neelie Kroes is 'outraged' by Uber ban in Belgium [Update]," The Next Web, Apr. 15, 2014, http://thenextweb.com/eu/2014/04/15/european-commission-vice-president-neelie-kroes-says-shes-outraged-uber-ban-belgium/.
3. Id.
4. Orly Lobel, The Law of the Platform, Univ. of San Diego, Legal Studies Research Paper Series, Mar. 2016, available at http://ssrn.com/abstract = 2742380.

Periodical and Internet Sources Bibliography

The following articles have been selected to supplement the diverse views presented in this chapter.

Le Chen, Alan Mislove, and Christo Wilson, "Peeking Beneath the Hood of Uber," *IMC '15 Proceedings of the 2015 ACM Conference on Internet Measurement Conference*, October 28, 2015.

Koen Frenken, Toon Meelen, Martijn Arets and Pieter van de Glind, "Smarter Regulation for the Sharing Economy," *Guardian*, May 20, 2015. https://www.theguardian.com/science/political -science/2015/may/20/smarter-regulation-for-the-sharing -economy.

John J. Horton and Richard J. Zeckhauser, "Owning, Using, and Renting: Some Simple Economics of the "Sharing Economy" National Bureau of Economic Research, February 2016. http:// www.nber.org/papers/w22029.

Alberto Marchi and Ellora-Julie Parekh, "How the Sharing Economy Can Make Its Case," *McKinsey Quarterly*, December 2015. http:// www.mckinsey.com/business-functions/strategy-and-corporate -finance/our-insights/how-the-sharing-economy-can-make-its -case.

Sofia Ranchordas, "Does Sharing Mean Caring? Regulating Innovation in the Sharing Economy," *Minnesota Journal of Law, Science and Technology (Winter 2015)*, September 7, 2014. ssrn .com/abstract=2492798.

Will Yakowicz, "Will the Uberization of Business Models Kill the Economy?," Inc.com. http://www.inc.com/will-yakowicz/serious -business-sharing-economy-good-or-bad.html.

Georgios Zervas, Davide Proserpio, and John Byers, "The Rise of the Sharing Economy: Estimating the Impact of Airbnb on the Hotel Industry," Boston University School of Management Research Paper, No. 2013-16, February, 2014. Papers.ssrn.com/sol3/papers .cfm?abstract_id=2366898.

OPPOSING
VIEWPOINTS®
SERIES

CHAPTER 3

Who Benefits from the Sharing Economy?

Chapter Preface

The question of who benefits from the sharing economy is one with several possible answers, all of which are likely correct. It's also one with the potential to start a memorable—and heated—debate. There's plenty of evidence to show that people working in the sharing economy are reaping rewards from it, and equal evidence to show that consumers of these goods and services are also benefitting. However, evidence to the contrary—that people working in the sharing economy are being exploited—is also strong, and presents several new layers of fodder for discussion.

The argument that there's a strong need for labor protections for employees in this newer economy is prevalent, as is the point that regulations on these fronts need to be developed sooner rather than later. Several researchers and experts have voiced concerns that workers' wages suffer under their employers' need for profit, and that those corporations are, ultimately, the ones who benefit.

If they're getting a great deal, then yes, customers benefit. Perhaps they're able to stay in a city whose hotels would be cost prohibitive or attend an event that they can now get to quite easily. On the flip side, however, what kind of recourse do the customers have if they're unhappy with the goods or services they've received? And what happens to the businesses—and middle men—they have left behind in this new age of peer-to-peer transactions? One author refers to disintermediation as "a posh word for cutting out the middle man," and points out that this strategy is nothing new, but that the internet's ability to enable "mass peer-to-peer connectivity" has brought it to the forefront.

The following chapter examines who does—and does not—benefit from the sharing economy. It takes into account several perspectives, including the businesses themselves, the employees, the consumers, the competition, the more conventional versions of said businesses, and the impact that each of these has on the others.

| *"Whether companies like this new approach or not wholly depends on whether they are part of the old or new economy."*

The Peer-to-Peer Economy Doesn't Benefit Workers

Robin Chase

In the following viewpoint, Robin Chase argues that as times change and the types of work available to the labor force shift, so must the way benefits are determined. While traditional jobs may offer benefits like paid time off, regular paychecks, and health insurance, Chase cites examples of individuals making a living from the sharing economy, which she calls the peer-to-peer economy, and questions the sustainability of their work and income structure. Chase is the cofounder and former CEO of Zipcar and the author of Peers, Inc.

As you read, consider the following questions:

1. According to this viewpoint, for how long has industrial capitalism set the tone for business in the United States?
2. According to this viewpoint (at the time of its publication), what percentage of jobs were freelance?
3. According to the author, rather than being tied to jobs, benefits should be tied to what?

"Who Benefits from the Peer-to-Peer Economy?" by Robin Chase, *Harvard Business Review*, July 28, 2015. Reprinted by permission.

Elizabeth Ann Berwick drove for Uber for eight weeks in 2014. She, and two others, then brought suit against the company. On June 16, the California Labor Commission ruled that she as a driver should have been classified as an employee – not an independent contractor – and that she was due over $4,000 in expenses and penalties. As expected, Uber filed its rebuttal on July 9, bolstered with written statements from more than 400 drivers supporting the company.

Are Uber drivers being exploited or fairly compensated? Should governments, consumers, and voters support or suppress the movement towards increasingly freelance labor? It depends.

The 150-year history of industrial capitalism has led the US (and others) to tie benefits and workplace rules to full-time employment. "Choose the full-time job with benefits!" parents urge their children.

Yet, in countries with national health benefits, free childcare, low-cost higher education, and robust social safety nets, working as an independent freelancer is great, and it is easier than ever with new, Internet-enabled platforms.

Jamie, who lives in France, sells handmade stationery on Etsy while working part-time as a family therapist. "I cannot imagine working for someone else. Being my own boss affords me the independence and flexibility I need to express my creative processes, be they typically artistic or intellectually creative. I am not tied down to other people's wants and expectations and can choose the paths I want or need to focus on at any particular stage in my life."

Sidney, who was working as an Uber driver in New York City when we met, told me that he loved being able to control the amount of money he'd earn in a week. If he needed $400 to cover rent, then he'd work the necessary hours to earn it. He told me if you were smart and hardworking, working for yourself was the only way to go. Yet I worried that his calculus didn't include the full costs of the car, or factor in sick and vacation days, health insurance, or the inevitable retirement that stretched ahead.

In the End, Customers Are the Winners

Seemingly overnight, the so-called "sharing economy" has turned traditionally underused assets into competitors to established industries. Some believe this business model will threaten incumbents across the economy. How widespread the sharing economy will be remains to be seen, but to date it has had unquestionably large effects on the hotel industry through Airbnb and the taxi industry through ride-sharing services like Uber, Lyft, and Sidecar. The development of new services that did not previously exist almost by definition make consumers better off. The benefits to consumers, however, are likely to extend beyond those who use these new services if incumbents are forced to respond to new competition by improving service and/or reducing price.

The rapid growth of ride-sharing has upended the taxicab industry, which is traditionally heavily regulated. Incumbents' most prominent reactions have been to lobby regulators to slow the growth of ride-sharing. They might, however, also try to retain customers by competing for them in the market. However, regulations limit incumbents' set of potential competitive responses. Prices are regulated and change infrequently while taxi drivers cannot, on their own, reduce prices or offer the frictionless payment systems ride-sharing services use. Even so, drivers might respond by trying to offer higher quality rides than they used to provide. Improved quality might take the form of, for example, being more courteous to passengers by turning off the radio, not talking on a cell phone while driving, and so on. The difficulty of signalling this quality to a potential passenger and lack of repeat business blunts this incentive, but with less business taxi drivers may behave better in the hopes of bigger tips or to reduce the chances that a passenger will complain. If ride-sharing has generated this kind of competitive response by taxis then even consumers who do not use ride-sharing may benefit.

"The Competitive Effects of the Sharing Economy: How Is Uber Changing Taxis?" by Scott Wallsten, June 1, 2015.

This new way of working also rewards the ambitious, the hardworking, and the entrepreneurial, and it moves us closer to a real meritocracy. Our résumés become irrelevant, and we can try our hands at many things and more quickly figure out what we want to do more of. In the famous *New Yorker* cartoon, a dog seated at a computer says to another one looking on, "On the Internet, nobody knows you're a dog." We've moved beyond that. With the rise of social networks (and expectation of NSA-level spying), it's become more true that "everyone knows you're a dog, and nobody cares." It's your work product and your reputation that matter.

According to Economic Modeling Specialists International, the number of freelance workers in the U.S. grew from 20 million in 2001 to 32 million in 2014. Freelance work now comprises almost 18 percent of all jobs. This trend is expanding explosively. And not just because workers are unemployed or unable to make ends meet with traditional jobs (although this has some truth in it) but also because companies are finding it advantageous to rely on freelance labor.

It used to be that companies would gain a competitive edge by bringing more and more people, assets, and resources inside the company in order to reduce transaction costs. The Internet has stripped that advantage away. Now, the smartest companies are using the Internet's ability to facilitate collaboration by leveraging assets, resources, and expertise outside of their sphere of control. I call this new collaboration "Peers Inc." and we are seeing its transformative and disruptive power in every sector of the economy.

As early as 2000, Zipcar (which I co-founded) built a platform that empowered its members to do work that used to be done by car rental employees. The platforms created by Uber and Lyft (who invented the idea) have redefined what it means to be a taxi and a taxi driver, and Airbnb has done the same with hotels and hoteliers. The effect extends well beyond what has been called the "sharing economy" – featuring many instances of peer-to-peer coordination of the use of assets — to what I think of as the collaborative economy: marked by many platforms that engage a diversity of peers to contribute excess capacity which can be harnessed for greater impact.

Massive Open Online Courses (MOOCs) are challenging work flows in the education sector. 3D printing will restructure manufacturing. The music and print media – in fact, all content producers – have had to transform as new platforms increasingly give the small the powers of marketing and distribution that were once reserved for the very large.

Companies like these, who tap directly into the full diversity and energy of their human marketplaces, are able to scale faster, learn faster, innovate and adapt faster. Whether companies like this new approach or not wholly depends on whether they are part of the old or new economy.

Governments need to recognize and prepare for this new third way of working which is neither full-time nor temporary part-time, but a new way of life. The Internet exists and everything that can become a platform will. Local and federal governments need to start tying benefits to people and not jobs, ensuring that labor is protected during this disruptive and swift transition.

In a world struggling to cope with incessant disruption brought on by fast-paced technical innovation, climate change, urbanization, and globalization, *Peers, Inc.* is the structure for our times. It enables us to experiment, iterate, adapt, and evolve at the required pace. I'm happy this flexible new tool has come to exist. But while we are reaping the economic benefits brought on by individual contributions, we need to proactively share the productivity and innovation gains with individuals, too.

"If this form of innovation grows significantly, the sharing economy may come to transform the world of work."

The Sharing Economy Isn't Likely to Hurt Capitalism

Chris Martin

In the following viewpoint, Chris Martin points out that research on the sharing economy is scarce, and he reveals his findings from a study of about 250 sharing-economy-related articles and reports. After considering a range of views from advocates and critics alike, he devised four possible paths for the sharing economy: Consumption 2.0, new ways of working, a fair and sustainable future, and fading away. Martin is an environmental social scientist at the University of Manchester.

As you read, consider the following questions:

1. According to the author, what is Consumption 2.0?
2. According to this viewpoint, what does economic journalist Paul Mason believe could end as a result of the sharing economy?
3. What is the author concerned the sharing economy will do to quality of life, according to this viewpoint?

The sharing economy could bring about the end of capitalism: that's the provocative claim made by economic journalist Paul Mason, among others. But my ongoing research indicates that there are many possible futures for the sharing economy: it could transform the world of work as we know it – or it could gradually fade from the public eye.

The exact nature and impacts of the sharing economy are still disputed. The organisers of social movements, entrepreneurs, established businesses and politicians all have very different ideas of what the sharing economy is, and what it should become. For example, Share the World's Resource (a not-for-profit civil organisation) talks about building a sharing economy based on "shared" public services, which are funded by taxation.

Meanwhile, the UK government speaks of building a sharing economy based on online peer-to-peer platforms, which enable citizens to become micro-entrepreneurs by renting out assets such as homes, driveways and pets. So it seems that a diverse range of actors can see their own hopes, fears and values reflected in the sharing economy. But one thing is for sure: online platforms such as Airbnb and Uber have grown from Silicon Valley startups to global corporations, and this trend will probably continue.

Research on the economic, environmental and social impacts of these enterprises is scarce. As a result, there is very little evidence to help us understand how the sharing economy will develop. So I analysed approximately 250 sharing-economy-related articles and reports, which contained contrasting views from advocates and critics. Based on this evidence, I mapped out four possible paths for the sharing economy: and only one of them predicts that the sharing economy will bring capitalism to its knees, as Mason holds.

Consumption 2.0

Some have argued that online sharing platforms can enable a new form of collaborative consumption, where citizen access rather than own products. For example, peer-to-peer car sharing platforms,

Benefits for Low-Income Consumers

In his recent work, Sundararajan and coauthor Samuel Fraiberger analyzed two years of data from Getaround, a peer-to-peer car-sharing platform in San Francisco. Their model suggests that consumer well-being improves as these types of marketplaces expand. The benefits were up to three times greater for lower-income consumers. That's partly because people are able to consume goods that were previously unaffordable. Sharing services also allow people to use their assets more efficiently—for example, by renting out their cars or spare rooms. People who switch from owning to renting, meanwhile, benefit from lower costs.

The economic impacts are broad. The sharing economy not only helps people monetize their underused assets but also lowers the barriers to entrepreneurialism. In fact, Sundararajan noted that many of these companies sprang up during the Great Recession.

"Sharing Economy Boosts Consumer Well-Being, Expert Says," by Arun Sundararajan, Federal Reserve Bank of Atlanta (FRB Atlanta), 2015.

such as Easycar Club, enable individuals to rent out their car to others when they are not using it.

The idea is that these new forms of consumption have major environmental benefits. As these practices reduce consumer demand for products, this in turn reduces the number of products manufactured and ultimately decreases carbon emissions. If this form of innovation grows significantly, the sharing economy may enable a new form of consumption.

But this path seems unlikely to be transformative: simply using products more efficiently will not, on its own, lead to a sustainable economy. By engaging in more efficient forms of consumption within the sharing economy, people save money, which they then spend on other carbon intensive other products and services. For example, someone using a car sharing platform could spend the money they save on holiday flights, thereby increasing their overall carbon emissions.

New ways of working

Much of the interest in the sharing economy – particularly in the United States – focuses on online platforms which enable citizens to engage in new forms of work. For example, Uber enables car-owners with "spare" time to work as taxi-drivers. Airbnb enables property owners with "spare" space to work as hoteliers or landlords. Taskrabbit enables anyone with "spare" time to perform tasks including cleaning, shopping and other domestic errands. These platforms enable consumers (for instance, a tourist) and service providers (an Airbnb host) to form short-term relationships.

But sharing economy workers do not automatically have access to the rights and benefits of contracted employees, such as sick pay and annual leave. And as the recent swathe of cases brought against Uber and its contemporaries has shown, there is strong opposition to these conditions on behalf of the workers themselves, and those they compete with.

If this form of innovation grows significantly, the sharing economy may come to transform the world of work. But whether you view this a path to creating new opportunities for entrepreneurship, or promoting the exploitation of low-skilled or low-income workers, rather depends on your political beliefs and values.

A fair and sustainable future

Paul Mason is not alone in predicting that the sharing economy will bring an end to capitalism. Radical grassroots actors such as Ouishare and Shareable, who are critical of the capitalist economic system, are creating a sharing economy built upon the principles of collaboration, sustainability and equality.

They talk about a sharing economy of grassroots activities, ranging from cooperatives, to open source software and hardware, to crowdfunding, to the maker movement – a social movement which enables individuals to create products, challenging the dominant systems of large-scale industrial manufacturing.

This vision includes grassroots innovations as diverse as bread co-ops, open-source communities developing tools for reducing energy demand, Kickstarter and Fab Labs, which provide people with access to the tools needed to manufacture products.

These activities share a focus on empowering communities and creating a decentralised, sustainable economic system. If these diverse forms of innovation grow significantly then the sharing economy may, indeed, bring about the end of capitalism.

Fading away

Given the diverse visions of the sharing economy, it's questionable whether the idea will stand the test of time. It's possible that the sharing economy will lose meaning as a concept and gradually disappear from public, media and policy discussions.

Perhaps it will be replaced by concepts such as the gig economy – referring to platforms enabling new forms of work – or the collaborative economy – referring to grassroots action to create a more sustainable economy.

It's hard to tell which path we're currently on. I for one hope Mason is right, and that the sharing economy will bring an end to an unsustainable system. But I fear that it's more likely to transform the world of work in a negative way, reducing quality of life for many within society. The people championing this path are those with great power within the capitalist economy.

Meanwhile, those advocating for a path towards a more equal economy – such as grassroots organisations – are currently marginalised and disempowered. It's clear who the odds will favour.

> *"Given Uber's size, power, and ambitions, whether lawmakers ensure that it advances those values may shape the future of low-wage work."*

Uber Shifts the Responsibility—and Potential Benefits—to Drivers

Brishen Rogers

In the following excerpted viewpoint, Brishen Rogers argues that Uber drivers have some unique opportunities—some beneficial and others detrimental—at the infancy of the transportation company. Rogers notes that it is especially challenging for Uber drivers to protect themselves against discrimination. On the other hand, he argues that they have a technological likelihood of being able to easily organize and affect change regarding labor standards. Finally, the author discusses what impact Uber may have on markets that are currently peripheral to its services, like delivery and pickup of goods. Rogers is a professor of law at Temple University's James E. Beardsley School of Law.

As you read, consider the following questions:

1. According to this viewpoint, what responsibility is given to drivers in order for them to remain in good standing with Uber?

2. According to this viewpoint, what factors may contribute to Uber drivers' ability to organize regarding labor standards?

3. According to the author, what will ultimately drive which low-wage jobs are saved?

C. Discrimination

Discrimination seems to be a risk of Uber's rider-feedback model, which requires drivers to maintain a minimum score or be kicked off the service. Passengers may give bad reviews to racial-minority drivers, whether out of implicit or explicit bias. Drivers in turn may be less likely to pick up riders if they learn that they are racial minorities and may generally prefer to pick up or drop off clients in wealthier, whiter neighborhoods.

But of course Uber did not invent discrimination against riders. Taxi drivers' discrimination against black men in particular is notorious.[38] Taxis also regularly refuse to accept fares to poor neighborhoods, even when doing so is clearly illegal. In fact, Uber drivers may in some cases be more likely to drive to or pick up in poor neighborhoods.[39] Cabs' refusal to do so may reflect their difficulty in finding return fares. Uber's matching app could mitigate that problem.

More importantly, Uber's data collection could enable it to deter or prevent discrimination by drivers—which is quite difficult in a fractured taxi industry. Whether Uber ultimately takes that step will depend in part on the answers to two threshold legal questions. First, Uber's exact duties under federal and state civil rights laws are not yet clear.[40] Disability-rights organizations have argued that the company is a taxi service under the Americans with Disabilities Act of 1990,[41] for example, and therefore must make reasonable accommodations for disabled passengers.[42] Uber disagrees, but the Justice Department has sided with the plaintiffs in that case.[43] Second, if Uber drivers are not Uber employees, the company's vicarious liability for discrimination by drivers may be limited—though as the Justice Department noted, "while an entity may contract out its service, it may not contract away its ADA responsibilities."[44]

Even if courts side with the company, however, Congress or state legislatures could simply clarify that ride-sharing companies are public accommodations, thus holding them responsible if they fail to take reasonable steps to prevent discrimination by drivers.[45] Such steps might include hiding race, disability, and home-address data from drivers, implementing internal policies against such discrimination, and developing algorithms to determine which drivers regularly refuse fares from minority riders. The EEOC and state attorneys general could also encourage Uber down this path even if they cannot order it there, and given Uber's public visibility, antidiscrimination norms may have similar effects even absent law reforms. Traditional cab companies that lack Uber's data pool and public profile are both less susceptible to public pressure and less capable of implementing such compliance programs.

Uber's data pool could also help it to root out or correct for discrimination against drivers by passengers, which, to be fair, is not an obvious problem in the traditional cab sector. Federal law prohibits Uber from intentionally discriminating against drivers on the basis of race, even if they are contractors rather than employees.[46] Demonstrating intent is not easy, though, especially if Uber takes action against drivers based on biased customer feedback.[47]

But here again, a small tweak to federal or state law could do a great deal of work. Title VII[48] already prohibits discrimination by employment agencies, defined as persons or entities "regularly undertaking . . . to procure employees for an employer."[49] This does not apply to Uber, since riders are not drivers' employers. But since Uber performs a similar function in matching riders with drivers, Congress or state legislatures could revise employment discrimination statutes to classify ride-sharing services as employment agencies. Again, regulators could also press the company to ensure that its standards do not have such a disparate impact in the first place, and antidiscrimination norms may have a powerful disciplining effect.

There is another cost lurking here that deserves mention: Uber's rating system may require drivers, and perhaps even passengers, to engage in what has been called "emotional labor," or the work of establishing "micro-relationships that make customers feel good."[50] To stay above a certain rating, drivers may need to be friendly, and perhaps a bit servile. Cab drivers, in comparison, can afford to be themselves—which may involve venting their frustration at long hours and low pay. Such emotional labor may impose a disparate burden on racial minorities.[51] Minority drivers, to retain high ratings, may need to overcome white passengers' preconceptions, which can involve "identity work," or a conscious effort to track white, middle-class norms.[52] As argued in Part III, this may be a harbinger of things to come in the low-wage labor market.

D. Labor Standards

Finally, what about labor standards? One writer recently spoke for many when he argued that "'[s]haring economy' companies like Uber shift risk from corporations to workers, weaken labor protections, and drive down wages."[53] But this is not entirely accurate. As noted above, those standards are hardly ideal to begin with in the United States.[54] Rather than "shifting" risk onto workers, Uber may well be creating a new market, with a new allocation of risk and reward. How much risk drivers will bear, and what rewards they will enjoy, are very much open questions.

Granted, early signs are not encouraging for workers. For example, the company often acts unilaterally toward its drivers, changing terms and conditions at will, even when drivers have invested in cars in reliance on Uber's policies.[55] It is also the subject of lawsuits alleging that it misled drivers and the public by stating that 20 percent tips were built into fares and arguing that Uber drivers are actually employees and therefore eligible for reimbursement for employment-related expenses such as gas and insurance. In one such suit, a federal judge in California denied Uber's motion for summary judgment on the issue of employment status.[56]

I'm skeptical, though, that many courts will find Uber drivers to be employees. The test under most federal and state employment statutes is whether the putative employer has the right to control the work in question.[57] The most analogous recent cases, in which courts have split, involve FedEx drivers. Those that found for the workers have noted, for example, that FedEx requires uniforms and other trade dress, that it requires drivers to show up at sorting facilities at designated times each day, and that it requires them to deliver packages every day.[58] Uber drivers are different in each respect. They use their own cars, need not wear uniforms, and most importantly they work whatever hours they please.[59]

Such cases aside, Uber's consolidation of the sector may create opportunities for drivers to force better standards through collective action, and for regulators to ensure decent treatment of drivers. Associations of Uber drivers have already sprung up, calling attention to the long hours, low pay, and precariousness that they face.[60] In response to a work stoppage by the New York association, the company backed down from a plan to require drivers for its upscale UberBlack service to accept some lowercost fares from its cheaper UberX service.[61]

A couple factors suggest that drivers may continue to win such fights. Uber drivers are naturally tech savvy, and they may be able to organize cheaply using social media and other online platforms. Ride-sharing companies also appear to be competing for drivers. Gett, for example, has begun guaranteeing higher salaries as a means of recruitment,[62] indicating that drivers already enjoy a fair amount of bargaining power. Uber's consolidation of and leadership of the sector also make it a natural target for workers, since it can change their pay by fiat. Forcing change in the cab sector is arguably much harder, at least in cities with dispersed license ownership and multiple contractual intermediaries.

But some other factors suggest less cause for optimism. Uber drivers probably lack the sorts of communal ties that often enable worker organizing. They do not gather at a central dispatch location, and many work part-time and are unlikely to know other drivers. Drivers who speak out or strike also take enormous risks. Assuming that they are independent contractors, Uber could lawfully retaliate against drivers for striking under federal labor law.[63] While Uber has pledged not to do so, it is constrained at this point largely by public opinion, which is notoriously mercurial around labor issues.

Uber could also deploy sticks rather than carrots. It might, for example, insert a noncompete clause into its driver contracts, thus prohibiting drivers from working for other ride-sharing companies.[64] While such clauses are difficult to enforce in some states, including California, other states have enforced them even against independent contractors. That may deter drivers from leaving Uber regardless of enforceability.[65] Uber may also wield the possibility of shifting to driverless cars to prevent drivers from organizing,[66] and given its past behavior toward adversaries, there is little reason to think it will not do so when feasible.

Uber's ultimate effect on labor standards is therefore unclear. If its market share and network continue to grow, and its app enables drivers to have passengers rather than empty cars most of the time, it may be able to pay drivers well while keeping costs down. Or it may cut driver pay, or even cut drivers entirely, especially if price competition from other ride-sharing services heats up. As with most labor questions, which scenario unfolds will be determined as much by politics as by economics.

III. UBER AND THE FUTURE OF LOW-WAGE WORK

This is where Uber's rise begins to have unsettling implications. After the ride-sharing drivers' jobs are eliminated, what happens to mail- and package-delivery drivers whom Uber also hopes to displace?[67] What happens to supermarket clerks and other retail clerks as more and more shopping goes online, with goods delivered by—yes—Uber? What happens to the fast-food workers displaced as Uber or some other "Internet of things" company delivers fast food on demand in driverless cars?

I do not know, of course, but I'll close with two observations. First, a society committed to freedom and equality might not actually want to save such jobs. Ideally, the stunning productivity gains promised by new technologies like Uber could reduce society's need for work that is deadening to the human spirit. But without far-reaching changes to our social safety net, doing so would render tens of millions destitute. I worry that such a crisis in the low-wage labor market is close on the horizon, and that society is unprepared to deal with it.

Second, I suspect that consumer demand rather than commitments to freedom and equality will ultimately determine which low-wage jobs are saved, with menial tasks performed by humans only when consumers prefer not to deal with machines. At that point, workers without many skills will find their access to work determined in part by their ability to smile and appear cheerful—to perform emotional labor. This has already occurred in retail, hospitality, and other customer-service sectors.[68] It may next occur in positions with less frequent customer contact, such as hotel and commercial-office cleaners, security guards, and hospital orderlies. Some workers will need to ape middleclass norms of sociability, others to defer to customers. Workers "hired" through Task Rabbit and other sharing-economy platforms may face similar incentives to engage in emotional labor, since those platforms—like Uber—require workers to maintain a certain feedback rating.[69] Metaphorically, more and more workers will be waiting tables.

Which brings us back to the public's mistrust of Uber. The company's name clearly evinces Nietzsche's vision of a new morality and a new class dedicated to human excellence.[70] But in Uber executives' hands, that ideal has become little more than a defense of privilege. The company's leaders seem just fine with a future in which the many are supplicant to the few, and the few are licensed to disregard ordinary rules. Uber's slogan— "Everyone's private driver"—speaks volumes. Perhaps the public's intuitive skepticism toward Uber reflects a widespread sense that our economy should reflect basic democratic values. Given Uber's size, power, and ambitions, whether lawmakers ensure that it advances those values may shape the future of low-wage work.

Endnotes

38 See, for example, Russ Ptacek, Hidden Camera DC Taxi Investigation Documents Blacks Waiting Longer and 25% Stranded in Favor of Whites (WUSA May 22, 2013), online at http://www.wusa9.com/news/article/241642/373/Undercover-Probe-25-Of -Taxi... (visited Feb 26, 2015).

39 See, for example, Latoya Peterson, Cab Drivers, Uber, and the Costs of Racism (Racialicious Nov 28, 2012), online at http://www.racialicious.com/2012/11/28/cab -drivers-uber-and-the-costs-of... (visited Feb 26, 2015); Johana Bhuyiyan, Uber and Lyft Position Themselves as Relief from Discrimination (Buzzfeed Oct 7, 2014), online at http://www.buzzfeed.com/johanabhuiyan/app-based-car-services-may-reduce-... (visited Feb 26, 2015) (noting that Uber's policy that drivers must accept 90 percent of all requests has the potential to reduce racial profiling and destination bias).

40 Compare 42 USC § 2000a(b) (defining "place of public accommodation" to include, for example, hotels and motels, restaurants, and theaters, but not transportation companies), with 49 CFR § 37.29 ("Providers of taxi service are subject to the requirements of [the transportation and related provisions of Titles II and III of the ADA]."); DC Code § 2-1401.02(24) (defining "place of public accommodation" to include "all public conveyances").

41 Pub L No 101-336, 104 Stat 327, codified as amended at 42 USC § 12101 et seq.

42 See Complaint for Violations of the Americans with Disabilities Act, 42 U.S.C. § 12101 et seq., the California Unruh Civil Rights Act, Cal. Civ. Code §§ 51 & 52, and the California Disabled Persons Act, Cal. Civ. Code §§ 54–54.3, National Federation of the Blind of California v Uber Technologies, Inc, Case No 3:14-cv-4086, ¶¶ 52–75 at *14–20 (ND Cal filed Sept 9, 2014) (available on Westlaw at 2014 WL 4628579).

43 Bob Egelko, Obama Administration Takes Sides in Disability Suit against Uber (SFGate.com Dec 23, 2014), at http://www.sfgate.com/bayarea/article/Obama -administration-takes-sides-i... (visited Feb 26, 2015).

44 Statement of Interest of the United States of America, National Federation of the Blind of California v Uber Technologies, Inc, Case No 3:14-cv-4086, *5 (ND Cal filed Dec 23, 2014).

45 Just as employers are held liable when they fail to take reasonable steps to prevent and remedy hostile-work-environment harassment by employees. See Farragher v City of Boca Raton, 524 US 775, 805–06 (1998).

46 While Title VII does not protect non-employees, racial discrimination against independent contractors is illegal. See 42 USC § 1981. See also generally Runyon v McCrary, 427 US 160 (1976). Moreover, systemic disparate treatment claims are available under § 1981. See Alexander v Fulton County, Ga, 207 F3d 1303 (11th Cir 2000) (permitting the use of statistical evidence to prove discrimination).

47 For example, since disparate impact theory is not available under § 1981, see General Building Contractors Association v Pennsylvania, 458 US 375, 383 n 8 (2002), a policy that simply banned drivers who received below a certain passenger rating would not be actionable even if it led to more minority drivers being penalized.

48 Civil Rights Act of 1964, Pub L No 88-352, 78 Stat 241, codified in various sections of Title 42.

49 42 USC § 2000e(c).

50 Jedediah Purdy, Why Your Waiter Hates You (The Daily Beast Oct 26, 2014), online at http://www.thedailybeast.com/articles/2014/10/26/there-s-a-reason-your-w... (visited Feb 26, 2015). See also Paul Myerscough, Short Cuts (London Review of Books Jan 3, 2013), online at http://www.lrb.co.uk/v35/n01/paul-myerscough/short-cuts (visited Feb 26, 2015) (describing requirements of "affective labour" at Pret a Manger cafe).

51 See Nancy Leong, The Sharing Economy Has a Race Problem (Salon Nov 2, 2014), online at http://www.salon.com/2014/11/02/the_sharing_economy_has_a_race_problem (visited Feb 26, 2015).

52 See generally, for example, Devon Carbado, Acting White? Rethinking Race in Post-racial America (Oxford 2013).

53 Avi Asher-Schapiro, Against Sharing (*Jacobin* Sept 19, 2014), online at https://www.jacobinmag.com/2014/09/against-sharing (visited Feb 26, 2015). See also Dave Jamieson, Meet the Real Amazon Drones, Huffington Post Business (*Huffington Post* Apr 24, 2014), online at http://www.huffingtonpost.com/2014/04/24/amazon-delivery-lasership_n_519... (visited Feb 26, 2015) (noting that Amazon's contractors "shift[ ] the costs associated with employment away from the company and onto the worker").

54 The story is of course different in Germany, France, and England, where cab drivers earn middle-class salaries. See Rick Noak, Why Germany (and Europe) Fears Uber (*Wash Post* Sept 4, 2014), online at http://www.washingtonpost.com/blogs/worldviews/wp/2014/09/04/why-germany... (visited Feb 26, 2015).

55 See, for example, Odette Yousef, Cabbies Threaten to Abandon Uber over Changes (WBEZ Feb 3, 2014), online at http://www.wbez.org/news/cabbies-threaten-abandon-uber-over-changes-109625 (visited Feb 26, 2015).

56 O'Connor v Uber Technologies, Inc, 2013 WL 6354534, *5–7 (ND Cal).

57 See Mark A. Rothstein, Employment Law § 10.8 at 907–10 (West 4th ed 2010).

58 Compare In re FedEx Ground Package System, Inc, Employment Practices Litigation, 758 F Supp 2d 638, 658–60 (ND Ind 2010) (finding that FedEx drivers are independent contractors, albeit with some state law exceptions), with Wells v FedEx Ground Package System, Inc, 979 F Supp 2d 1006, 1024 (ED Mo 2013) (finding that FedEx drivers are employees).

59 They may fare better under Massachusetts' liberalized test for employment status, which requires a putative employer to prove that a worker is an independent contractor

60 The most prominent is probably the California App-Based Driver's Association. See generally California App-Based Driver's Association, online at http://www.cadateamsters .org/aboutus.php (visited Feb 26, 2015).

61 Alison Griswold, Uber Just Caved on a Big Policy Change after Its Drivers Threatened to Strike, Slate Moneybox Blog (*Slate* Sept 12, 2014), online at http://www.slate.com/blogs /moneybox/2014/09/12/uber_drivers_strike_they_... (visited Feb 26, 2015).

62 See Griswold, In Search of Uber's Unicorn (cited in note 4). See also We're Doubling Driver Pay. Permanently. (The Gett Blog Oct 15, 2014), online at http://gett.com /doublepay (visited Feb 26, 2015).

63 See Elizabeth Kennedy, Comment, Freedom from Independence: Collective Bargaining Rights for "Dependent Contractors", 26 Berkeley J Empl & Labor L 143, 152–53 (2005) (noting that the protections afforded by the National Labor Relations Act do not extend to independent contractors). See also id at 168–74 (discussing the interaction between independent contractor status and labor rights).

64 The company may already have incorporated such a clause into its driver contracts, though I suspect not. Given the visibility and unpopularity of noncompetes today, Uber organizers would likely have flagged it for reporters.

65 Ruth Simon and Angus Loten, Litigation over Noncompete Clauses Is Rising (*Wall St J* Aug 14, 2013), online at http://online.wsj.com/articles/SB1000142412788732344640457900 11501388418552 (visited Feb 26, 2015) ("California, where startups are plentiful, makes it particularly difficult to enforce such agreements.").

66 This change could have enormous positive safety and environmental effects. See Radhika Sanghani, Google's Driverless Cars Are 'Safer' Than Human Drivers (*The Telegraph* Oct 29, 2013), online at http://www.telegraph.co.uk/technology /google/10411238/Googles-driverless... (visited Feb 26, 2015); Driverless Cars Could Be Good for Environment (*Poughkeepsie J* June 8, 2014), online at http://www. poughkeepsiejournal.com/story/tech/science/environment/2014/0... (visited Feb 26, 2015). But see Bradley Berman, Why Driverless Cars Won't Save the Environment, Readwrite (*Business Insider* Dec 27, 2013), online at http://www.businessinsider.com /driverless-cars-environment-2013-12 (visited Feb 26, 2015).

67 For a discussion of Uber's attempts at entering the delivery market, see Doug Gross, Uber Gets into Delivery Game with Rush (CNN Apr 8, 2014), online at http://www.cnn .com/2014/04/08/tech/mobile/uber-rush-delivery (visited Feb 26, 2015).

68 See generally, for example, Hyun Jeong Kim, Hotel Service Providers' Emotional Labor: The Antecedents and Effects on Burnout, 27 *Intl J Hospitality Mgmt* 151 (2008); Blake E. Ashforth and Ronald H. Humphrey, Emotional Labor in Service Roles: The Influence of Identity, 18 *Acad Mgmt Rev* 88 (1993).

69 See, for example, TaskRabbit Community Guidelines: Performance Standards Compliance (TaskRabbit Aug 27, 2013) online at https://taskrabbit.zendesk.com /entries/22295495-TaskRabbit-Community-Gui... (visited Feb 26, 2015).

> "The uniqueness of this new sharing economy is that it mobilizes technology, markets, and the 'wisdom of crowds' to bring strangers together."

The Sharing Economy Isn't Solving Labor Problems

Juliet Schor

In the following excerpted viewpoint, Juliet Schor argues that the sharing economy may perpetuate—or at the least, not mitigate—class, gender, and racial biases and hierarchies. She questions whether these sites build relationships and trust, as they sometimes suggest they do (or will), and also points to weaknesses in a system that should have high standards when it comes to labor conditions. Schor is a sociologist and author of the 1992 bestseller The Overworked American.

As you read, consider the following questions:

1. According to the author, what is "stranger sharing"?
2. According to the viewpoint, what is "sharewashing"?
3. What are some factors cited by the author that determine how much value providers on these platforms can capture?

Does the Sharing Economy Build Social Capital?

While the discourse of novelty in this sector is overrated, there is something new afoot: what I call "stranger sharing." Although there are exceptions (e.g., elite travelers in ancient Greece), people have historically limited sharing to within their own social networks. Today's sharing platforms facilitate sharing among people who do not know each other and who do not have friends or connections in common. Stranger sharing entails higher degrees of risk, and many of today's exchanges are quite intimate—sharing one's home or car, going into strangers' homes to do work, or eating food prepared by unknown cooks. The platforms reduce risk by posting information on users via feedback and ratings. This points to a second novel dimension—the use of digital technology to reduce transactions costs, create opportunities in real time, and crowdsource information. The uniqueness of this new sharing economy is that it mobilizes technology, markets, and the "wisdom of crowds" to bring strangers together.

Many sites in the sharing space advertise social connection as a core outcome of their activity. But do these sites actually build friendships, networks, and social trust? The evidence is mixed. Stanford sociologist Paolo Parigi and his colleagues have found that Couchsurfing does, in fact, lead to new friendships. However, the ability of the platform to create such connections, especially close ones, has declined since its inception in 2003. Users have become "disenchanted" as the relationships they form are now more casual and less durable.[14] Other studies have found that social connection can be elusive, with time bank participants expressing disappointment in the degree of social connection they gained and RelayRides users describing their interactions as "anonymous" and "sterile."[15]

The role of ratings and reputational information is at the center of questions about social capital. The conventional wisdom is that the provision of crowdsourced information on users is what leads people to feel safe about interacting in intimate ways with strangers.[16] Parigi's research, however, uncovered a paradox: the more reputational information the site provided about people, the less users formed strong bonds. Venturing into unknown territory with strangers may be more of the appeal of some sites than their ability to master a utilitarian calculus of risk and reward.

Sharing economy sites can also reproduce class, gender, and racial biases and hierarchies. In our research at a food swap, my team and I found that cultural capital, a type of class privilege, limited the trades members were willing to make. Only participants with the "right" offerings, packaging, appearance, or "taste" received offers or, in some cases, even felt comfortable returning. In our time bank research, we found that some people screen potential trading partners by grammar and education, and that many highly educated people were unwilling to offer their most valuable skills (like programming or web design), preferring instead to act as amateur electricians or manual workers.[17] A recent study also reported evidence of racial discrimination among Airbnb users, finding that non-black hosts were able to charge 12% more than blacks for comparable properties.[18]

Exploiting Labor?

The debut of the sharing economy was marked by plenty of language about doing good, building social connections, saving the environment, and providing economic benefits to ordinary people. It was a feel-good story in which technological and economic innovation ushered in a better economic model. Especially in the aftermath of the financial crash, this positive narrative was hard to resist. Social activists flocked to these initiatives, hoping to piggyback on their popularity. Maybe, they thought, digital P2P platforms could be a pathway to a true grassroots, inclusive, fair, and lowimpact economy.

Dean Baker, a progressive economist, claims the new sharing is "largely based on evading regulations and breaking the law" and subjects consumers to a substandard, possibly unsafe product. [19] Anthony Kalamar has called out "sharewashing," in which platforms shift risk onto employees under the guise of "sharing."[20]

Tom Slee, writing in *Jacobin*, has challenged Airbnb's claim that its users are single individuals earning small amounts of extra money, finding that half the revenue generated in New York City accrues to hosts with multiple listings.[21]

The central theme of the critics is that for-profit platforms have coopted what began as a progressive, socially transformative idea. Are they right? Regarding regulation, insurance, and taxation, the platforms are mobilizing political support, and, my experience suggests that they seem to be generally accepting of the idea that some regulation is necessary. Because most of the action is at the local and state level, there is a great deal of variation. But the trend seems to be towards a light regulatory touch that will allow the platforms to operate and grow.

There is less clarity about how the platforms are affecting labor conditions. Critics see them as architects of a growing "precariat," a class on the precarious edge of economic security, and argue that the impetus for sharing is not trust, but desperation.[22] From the perspective of drivers, errand-runners, and hosts, they describe a race to the bottom, with risk-shifting from companies to individual "microentrepreneurs."

Part of the difficulty in assessing the impact of these new earning opportunities is that they are being introduced during a period of high unemployment and rapid labor market restructuring. Working conditions and protections are already being eroded, real wages are declining, and labor's share of national income in the US has declined to historic lows. If the labor market continues to worsen for workers, their conditions will continue to erode, and it will not be because of sharing opportunities. Alternatively, if labor markets improve, sharers can demand more of the platforms because they have better alternatives. The two effects will work in opposite directions: with destruction of demand for legacy businesses and growth for sharing companies.

We also need to consider the diversity of industries in which sharing platforms are operating. Some sectors are characterized by high rents that are easy to capture with disruptive technologies.

Consider taxis. The biggest impact is likely the erosion in the value of medallions, the licenses they must possess to operate, because these medallions yield pure rents. While drivers in conventional operations may be capturing some of this excess profit, they are already facing adverse market conditions and, in many places, earning low hourly wages, as they are forced to pay high leasing and other fees to the owners of the medallions and vehicles. Union members fare better, but could they do better with Uber? Many have switched in hopes that they can. So far, though, the results are mixed, in part because they face increasing competition from platforms like UberX and Lyft, on which drivers use their own cars. And early high returns have been reduced by Uber's fare cuts, which have led to driver protests and organizing efforts.

An online platform with a good rating system should improve labor conditions. Consider the market for home health aides, where agencies currently take an enormous fraction of hourly fees, sometimes more than half.[23] A P2P matching platform would take a lower fraction, enabling low-paid workers to earn considerably more and have more autonomy over which jobs they accept. Where owners, agencies, or other actors are extracting rents, P2P platforms should do what they claim—distribute value to consumers and producers and away from gatekeepers and rent extractors.

Ultimately, the question is about how much value providers on these platforms can capture. This depends partly on whether they can organize themselves, a question the next section will explore. But there is another dimension, which is whether there is competition among platforms. Will they come to monopolize a given space, as we have seen in the areas of search, social media, and retail (Google, Facebook, Amazon)? Or are these P2P enterprises different? What they are offering is software, insurance, ratings, and a critical mass of participants. These are functions that can be replicated. For example, if the volume of users continues to grow, then critical mass may be achievable on multiple platforms. The ratings systems are not yet very good, and there are already start-ups attempting to delink ratings from individual platforms. Insurance can also be unbundled. At the May conference, venture capitalist Brad Burnham predicted a coming round of cost-squeezing akin to the cost-squeezing that the start-ups are inflicting on legacy businesses. On the other hand, the more the platforms are backed by and integrated with the large corporations that dominate the economy, the more monopolized the sector will be, and the less likely value will flow to providers and consumers.

Endnotes

(15) Dubois, Schor, and Carfagna, op. cit.; Fenton, op. cit.

(16) Recent studies have found inaccuracies in ratings systems, especially the tendency to overrate positive features and under-report bad experiences. A colleague and I review recent studies in Juliet B. Schor and Connor Fitzmaurice, "Collaborating and Connecting: The Emergence of a Sharing Economy," in Handbook on Research on Sustainable Consumption, eds. Lucia Reisch and John Thogersen (Cheltenham, UK: Edward Elgar), 2015.

(17) Juliet B. Schor et al., "Paradoxes of Openness and Distinction in the Sharing Economy," Unpublished paper, Boston College, 2014.

(18) Benjamin Hardin and Michael Luca, "Digital Discrimination: The Case of Airbnb," Harvard Business School Working Papers, 2014.

(19) Dean Baker, "Don't Buy the 'Sharing Economy' Hype: Aibnb and Uber Are Facilitating Ripoffs," The Guardian, May 27, 2014, available at http://www.theguardian.com/commentisfree/2014/may/27/airbnb-uber-taxes-regulation.

(20) Anthony Kalamar, "Sharewashing is the New Greenwashing," OpEd News, May 13, 2013, available at http://www.opednews.com/articles/Sharewashing-is-the-New-Gr-by-Anthony-Kalamar-130513-834.html.

(21) Tom Slee, "Sharing and Caring," Jacobin Magazine, January 24, 2014, available at https://www.jacobinmag.com/2014/01/sharing-and-caring/.

(22) Kevin Roose, "The Sharing Economy Isn't About Trust, It's About Desperation," New York Magazine, April 24, 2014, available at http://nymag.com/daily/intelligencer/2014/04/sharing-economy-is-about-desperation.html.

(23) Jane Gross, "Home Health Aides: What They Make, What They Cost," New York Times, December 30, 2008, available at http://newoldage.blogs.nytimes.com/2008/12/30/home-health-aides-what-they-make-what-they-cost/.

> *"Can this new economy really create 'good jobs', or does it bring more of the same precarious work we keep hearing about?"*

True Sharing Platforms Are More Beneficial than Businesses in the Sharing Economy

Duncan McCann

In the following viewpoint, Duncan McCann argues that sharing is not actually what is happening on platforms such as Uber, Airbnb, and TaskRabbit. He cites examples of true online sharing communities such as those for couch surfers, freecyclers, and even tool sharers/lenders. He presents the idea of cooperative platforms and suggests that they could be more beneficial than businesses based on the so-called practice of sharing that are actually about capitalism. McCann is a researcher at the New Economics Foundation.

As you read, consider the following questions:

1. According to the author, what is it about many platforms in the sharing economy that makes them not true to the word "sharing"?
2. According to the author, who creates the content for sites like Facebook and YouTube?
3. According to the author, how has Airbnb affected the housing market in some cities, such as San Francisco?

Duncan McCann, "The Sharing Economy: The Good, the Bad and the Real," New Economics Foundation, December 10, 2015. Reprinted by permission.

Whether it's hailing a taxi, finding somewhere to stay on your travels or arranging help at home, new and sophisticated websites and apps are ripping up traditional business models.

Services such as Uber, Airbnb and TaskRabbit, where people offer their skills or assistance directly to others, have been described as being part of the "sharing economy" – something the House of Lords has launched an enquiry into and NEF's Josh Ryan-Collins recently discussed on BBC Radio 4's Today programme (00.23.45).

When sharing isn't really sharing

But if I offered to share my cake with you and then I charged you money for a slice, would I have really shared it with you at all? No: it would be selling.

I'm not sharing my house by letting it out on Airbnb, nor do I share a car when I use Uber. In both cases someone has developed a new way of connecting a customer with a service provider in a new easy tech-driven way.

How could anything where a monetary transaction is involved be part of a sharing economy? We need a better way of describing this new strand of innovation.

What is the real sharing economy?

The real sharing economy is where people genuinely do share skills, information, knowledge and/or assets with each other in a way that creates additional value for everyone. People are linked either geographically, by things like freecycle or tool lending libraries, or through an online community, like couchsurfing. These platforms allow people to connect with each other to exchange a good or a service without payment.

But these services, at the moment at least, are a tiny part of the wider online exchange market economy picture – and certainly not the part with over $12 billion invested in it this year.

SHARING IN MARKETS

There has been a lot of excitement recently over what many people call the "sharing economy," in which new firms such as Uber, Lyft, Airbnb and other website businesses are increasing the value of capital assets. Uber and Lyft allow people to make productive use of their cars when they would otherwise be idle by quickly connecting with strangers desiring a ride. Airbnb makes it easy for those who have unused housing space to conveniently connect with those who desire accommodations. These firms are but three of a growing number that are creating, and making use of, new technologies, providing further evidence that entrepreneurial creativity is constantly coming up with new and unexpected ways to better serve consumers. The excitement over the sharing economy is fully justified.

Indeed, the enthusiasm over the sharing economy is even more justified than many may realize. What is now seen as the sharing economy is really a continuation of a long history of sharing through markets that enriches all our lives. The sharing in markets takes place so continually and unintentionally that it is easy to take it for granted, with little thought or appreciation. The popularity of the term "sharing economy" provides a teachable moment for highlighting the pervasiveness of market sharing and why we would all be impoverished without it.

"The Huge Benefits of the Sharing Economy," by David Henderson, Liberty Fund, August 3, 2015.

The bad sharing economy

The best known examples of the sharing economy – the likes of Facebook, Youtube, Uber and Airbnb – are Silicon Valley based and funded technology companies that created new online platforms through which to exchange.

Although operating in very different marketplaces – many creating new ones – they all do one thing in common: extract most of the value created by the users as corporate revenue.

In the above cases the platforms themselves would be useless without their users creating videos, posting updates, providing their homes and apartments or cars.

Yet the platform operators' capture all of the user generated value. And these companies are not interested in sharing the marketplace that they have created. Indeed Uber and Airbnb appear to have explicit strategies to create monopolies.

PayPal co-founder Peter Thiel has written of how 'competition is for losers', which led the founder of Shareable, Neal Gorenflo, to call these bad examples 'Deathstar platforms' for their destructive capabilities.

Participating in these new ventures can make sense from an individual perspective, enabling people to earn extra money from skills or things that may be otherwise unused. But added together they pose wider macro-economic concerns.

Look at the impact on the San Francisco property market, where prices have sky-rocketed as people wishing to buy homes compete with a new breed of Airbnb entrepreneur. Or London's already congested roads, where estimates suggest Uber has led to an additional 10,000 cars.

And while those offering their services can get freedom by generating income when it's right for them, huge uncertainties come with not being directly employed and instead being at the mercy of the platform provider.

Can this new economy really create 'good jobs', or does it bring more of the same precarious work we keep hearing about?

The answer is especially unclear of Uber, where they engage in regulatory avoidance, risk-shifting onto drivers and lack of employee contractual obligations. Trade Unions were created to address these problems and NEF research has shown the broader value to the economy of their role in maintaining decent wages.

Saving the 'good'

To customers, many of these new platforms are more effective than what's been before them. But they have yet to demonstrate that they can meet the major challenges facing our economy.

We need to ensure these new businesses are not able to get around legislation. Seoul banned Uber, not to stop the sharing economy, but to foster it in way that really supports those who create the value, in this case drivers, as well as residents.

There are some encouraging signs of alternative models – 'cooperative platforms' – where information, profits and power are genuinely shared. Why shouldn't online taxi and bed and breakfast platforms be run by and for the benefit of the cities that need them?

Policy should encourage such developments. Subsidies, tax-breaks or legal advice on governance could be given to those running on a cooperative basis, or conversely, dis-incentives given to monopolistic business models like Uber and Airbnb.

Maybe then we can begin to really talk about a sharing economy.

Periodical and Internet Sources Bibliography

The following articles have been selected to supplement the diverse views presented in this chapter.

Daily Mail, "Sharing Economy Reshapes Markets as Complaints Rise," AFP, February 3, 2015. http://www.dailymail.co.uk/wires/afp/article-2939000/Sharing-economy-reshapes-markets-complaints-rise.html.

Tawanna R. Dillahunt and Amelia R. Malone, "The Promise of the Sharing Economy Among Disadvantaged Communities," ACM Human Factors in Computing Systems (CHI) 2015, April 18 – 23 2015, Seoul, Republic of Korea. http://dx.doi.org/10.1145/2702123.2702189.

Charles Green, "Trusting and Being Trusted in the Sharing Economy"*Forbes*, May 2, 2012. http://www.forbes.com/sites trustedadvisor/2012/05/02/trusting-and-being-trusted-in-the -sharing-economy/2/#3171c0906b5b.

Juho Hamar, Mimmi Sjöklint, and Antti Ukkonen, "The Sharing Economy: Why People Participate in Collaborative Consumption," Social Science Research Network, May 2013.

Steven Hill, "How the Sharing Economy Screws American Workers," *Huffington Post*, January 20, 2016. http://www .huffingtonpost.com/steven-hill/sharing-economy-american workers_b_9018724.html.

Giovanni Quattrone, Davide Proserpio, Daniele Quercia, Licia Capra, Mirco Musolesi, "Who Benefits from the Sharing Economy of Airbnb?" Cornell University Library, February 6, 2016. https://arxiv.org/abs/1602.02238.

Jacob Thebault-Spieker, Loren Terveen, and Brent Hecht, "Avoiding the South Side and the Suburbs: The Geography of Mobile Crowdsourcing Markets," Urban Environments CSCW 2015, March 14-18, 2015, Vancouver, BC, Canada.

Brad Tuttle, "Can We Stop Pretending the Sharing Economy is All About Sharing?" *Money,* September 11, 2014. http://time.com /money/2933937/sharing-economy-airbnb-uber-monkeyparking.

OPPOSING
VIEWPOINTS®
SERIES

CHAPTER 4

Is the Sharing Economy Here to Stay?

Chapter Preface

As consumers grow familiar with a new way of making purchases or, in this case, utilizing services by way of the sharing economy, the question of that new business model's staying power positions itself front and center in the minds of consumers, in the media, and in top executives' offices. Potential concerns range from how this newer economy will affect conventional businesses, to what safety issues consumers should place focus on, and even to what issues are not actually worth any substantial apprehension.

Within the sharing, or peer-to-peer economy, for example, safety concerns are many, particularly for users of ride-sharing services, like Uber and Lyft. The jury is out, however, on whether there is enough solid evidence to support the notion that these services are any more dangerous than traditional taxis.

We're also seeing smaller industries develop as a result of the growth of the sharing economy. For example, a subset of innovators and entrepreneurs are now among those purchasing homes or cars solely for use through platforms like Airbnb and Uber. And Airbnb's effect on traditional hotels, like Marriott, has already been felt for years.

From the public's need for new apps, to people's interest in managing (or improving) as many elements of their lives as possible with just a click or a tap, to convenience, to cost savings, the sharing economy feels like a part of our culture that is here to stay. However, that statement, largely a generalization, is not without its caveats. A big enough safety concern, security breach, or publicity disaster could slow down—or halt—the sharing economy's momentum.

However, the extent to which we're seeing efforts on the part of all levels of government to establish regulations for this multi-faceted industry are a clear sign that the sharing economy is becoming increasingly firmly established as part of our everyday life. The newsworthy and ongoing movements to protect both the sharing economy's workers and consumers are a clear indication of at least some level of permanence to this business model.

The following chapter examines the factors that are likely contributors in determining whether or not the sharing economy is, indeed, here to stay.

> *"Tracking incidents involving ride-booking drivers or passengers is difficult: not all law enforcement agencies collect information the same way and many do not specifically track crimes or incidents related to ride-hailing services."*

For Ride-Bookers, Safety Remains an Issue

Dan Russo and Maggie DeBlasis

In the following viewpoint, Dan Russo and Maggie DeBlasis argue that safety is a top—if not the top—concern for all involved when it comes to ride-booking (or ride-hailing, or ride-sharing) services. The authors cover ride-booking-related tragic crimes, including six murders in Michigan, that have led to stronger laws and regulations when it comes to background checks in this area. They also cover technological safety features that some industry insiders argue make these services safer than their conventional counterparts, like taxis and limo services. Russo and DeBlasis cover news for the Washington DC Capital News Service.

As you read, consider the following questions:

1. According to the authors, what ride-hailing service stated on its Greater Maryland website that it "is not a transportation provider"?
2. What are some of the safety features Uber provides that traditional ride services, like taxis, do not?
3. According to the authors, what did the background check for Michigan Uber driver Jason Brian Dalton, who was charged with several crimes including six counts of murder, turn up?

I n many parts of the country – and indeed, around the world – a ride-booking service is as close and easy to use as launching an app on a smartphone.

But after nearly unimpeded growth in an industry that didn't exist a decade ago, around 30 U.S. jurisdictions have passed new ride-hailing regulatory legislation, all in the hopes of making services like Uber and Lyft safer for passenger use.

The murders of six victims in Kalamazoo, Mich., in late February, while uncommonly tragic, magnified uncertainties that have faced the ride-hailing industry throughout its meteoric growth. At the top of the list is the safety of its passengers and drivers.

Ride-booking services like Uber and Lyft insist their technology, driver background checks, and two-way rating systems keep their patrons safe, but critics consider those factors and the insurance coverage – or lack thereof – to be the ultimate concern.

Of all the issues facing the ride-booking industry, as well as its competitor, the taxi and limousine services, safety is the paramount concern.

Safety concerns high in poll

In a national poll of 3,000 riders, 81 percent said safety was the chief factor when using either a taxi or a ride-hailing service like Uber or Lyft. The survey was conducted for a taxi-limousine trade association, but the data was collected by FrederickPolls, an Arlington, Va., firm.

SurveyMonkey data found that riders found ride-booking "makes lives easier, but can be seen as expensive and unsafe."

But industry defenders see the safety issue as overblown.

"There is little evidence that the sharing economy services are more dangerous than traditional taxis," Matthew Feeney, a policy analyst with the Cato Institute, wrote last year. Cato is a Washington-based libertarian think-tank that generally advocates less government regulation.

"In fact," Feeney said, "the ridesharing business model offers big safety advantages as far as drivers are concerned. In particular, ride-hailing's cash-free transactions and self-identified customers substantially mitigate one of the worst risks associated with traditional taxis: the risk of violent crime."

Empirical data, however, is lacking. Tracking incidents involving ride-booking drivers or passengers is difficult: not all law enforcement agencies collect information the same way and many do not specifically track crimes or incidents related to ride-hailing services.

Maryland law brings equivalent regulation to taxis

February's Michigan murders involving an Uber driver was a rare deadly case. But several less serious incidents have occurred in the District of Columbia-Maryland-Virginia area within the last three years, according to local police records and news reports examined by Capital News Service.

Maryland passed a law in July that essentially sets the same requirements for taxi services and ride-booking companies on insurance, licensing, and the handling of complaints by passengers.

The sponsor of the law, Sen. Bill Ferguson, D-Baltimore City, said it represented a compromise between state limo and taxi services and ride-booking companies that allows for innovation without risking consumers' safety.

"It creates a new, more flexible regulating scheme to appropriate and regulate ridesharing services in the state of Maryland," Ferguson said.

"Ridesharing is enormously popular and has been even when they were operating in more of a gray area," the lawmaker continued. "(The bill) was a fiercely opposed bill for two years and last year we spent a lot of time working with all the stakeholders – taxis and limos to thinking with insurance regulators and companies and by the end of session last year ... almost everybody was in favor of it."

Virginia laws, also enacted in 2015, are similar, requiring more in-depth driver background checks – though not fingerprinting, which both Uber and Lyft are fighting in some areas – and the possession of insurance policies.

Uber is not a taxi and vice versa

If anything, the new laws and incidents in the Washington region underscore the general uneasiness toward ride-booking in the industry across the United States, according to critics.

"What we've typically seen with Uber is that they have really only done the bare minimum as required by law when it comes to important issues like safety, background checks and insurance," said Harry Campbell, an Uber and Lyft driver who quit his job as an engineer to run his blog, TheRideshareGuy.com. Campbell has also written articles on the ride-hailing industry for outlets such as Buzzfeed, the *New York Times*, and *Huffington Post* Live.

Most recently, Uber agreed to pay Los Angeles and San Francisco a $25 million settlement in a lawsuit brought by the cities' district attorneys. TechCrunch reported that the lawsuit claimed the company was "charging a $4 fee for passengers being collected from or going to California airports (and prosecutors) found that the 'toll' wasn't being passed on to the airports..."

As a part of the settlement, Uber has also pledged to stop using certain language claiming that their background checks were top-tier.

"We've agreed not to use terms like 'safest ride on the road' or describe our background checks as 'the gold standard,'" the company said in a statement.

At the epicenter of the ride-hailing controversy lie three clear, but intertwining issues: the fundamental difference between ride-booking and the taxi industry; the ride-hailing company's accountability for their drivers' and passengers' safeties; and the uncertainty surrounding the ride-booking platform's sustainability as a business model.

Matchmaking service

Uber even has a disclaimer at the bottom of its Greater Maryland website that might surprise a lot of its users: "Uber is not a transportation provider."

The difference at a basic level is that taxi companies usually own their vehicles and employ their drivers, whereas services like Uber and Lyft merely provide a platform for riders and drivers to match and meet up.

"Certainly when I teach, I say Uber is a platform and they are a matchmaking service to make sure that people who want rides and people provide rides can find each other," said Joe Bailey, a professor in the University of Maryland's Robert H. Smith School of Business.

"But (Uber and similar services are) not the ones who own the vehicles or (are) providing the transportation service," he said.

Ride-booking industry defense

In an effort to address demands from federal, state, and municipal agencies for information about its operations, Uber, the leading ride-hailing company, released its first transparency report on April 12.

The report detailed the scope of data that state and federal agencies and law enforcement requested in the second half of 2015, which included information on 50 Uber drivers in Maryland.

Uber, a privately-held company, said it hoped that its report would open "a public debate about the types and amounts of information regulated services should be required to provide to their regulators, and under what circumstances." Uber alleged that information requests of digital companies often exceeded those of their offline, more traditional counterparts.

"In many cases [agencies] send blanket requests without explaining why the information is needed, or how it will be used," Uber said in a statement. "And while this kind of trip data doesn't include personal information, it can reveal patterns of behavior — and is more than regulators need to do their jobs."

Uber and the entire ride-hailing industry believe that they are being backed into a corner, attempting to balance the requests of regulatory agencies and public demands for improved safety features, while protecting customer privacy.

According to Uber's website, all Uber drivers undergo a pre-screening process, including a review of motor vehicle and criminal records, in order to become certified and get paid. The company also maintains a code of conduct for both drivers' and passengers' safeties.

Technological safety features

Uber spokeswoman Kaitlin Durkosh said that all transportation has its risks, but Uber offers technological safety features that its competitors don't.

"I think what people often forget is that, just a few years ago, being able to wait safely inside for your ride, knowing who your driver was and when your ride was arriving, didn't really exist," Durkosh said. "Furthermore, if you wanted to get somewhere in that moment of time, you probably had to go outside and either hail down a taxi or walk to find a bus or a Metro stop."

Aside from Uber's background checks, its technological safeguards include a GPS locator that tracks the service's car, communication with drivers that don't require users to provide their phone numbers, and the rider's ability to share the location, route, and estimated time of arrival with a friend or family member. The company's app also provides the driver's first name, photo, license plate number, and rating.

After both the driver and rider rate each other, Uber's 24-hour safety team reviews each report and looks into any incidents, Durkosh said, though the company's code of conduct insists that, in case of an emergency, the proper authorities be contacted first.

However, those safety measures don't always prevent incidents.

Crime incidents include six in Annapolis

The *Washington Post* reported in July 2014 that Ryan Simonetti, CEO of New York-based Convene, said he was "kidnapped" by an Uber driver in the nation's capital. According to his Twitter account, Simonetti said he was "held against (his) will, and involved in a high speed chase across state lines with police #Crazy." An Uber representative confirmed to The Post the driver no longer drives for the company.

In September 2014, the Courthouse News Service reported a Washington, D.C., man sued Uber after being stabbed six times by his driver the previous September.

An off-duty Uber driver admitted to having been drinking in June 2015 when he veered from his side of the road and ran into an oncoming car, killing a Gaithersburg, Md., woman driving, according to Washington's WJLA-TV.

Those are only three of at least 10 accounts of Uber drivers endangering or allegedly endangering their passengers in the Washington area since 2013, according to police and media reports. Most occurred in Northwest Washington, a handful were recorded in Northern Virginia, and six were reported in Annapolis in 2015, the first year the company serviced the city.

In late February, the Baltimore Sun reported that a convicted drug dealer on supervised release regularly used Uber to transport heroin in Southeast Baltimore. Drug Enforcement Administration agents said in a search warrant they believed the passenger to be moving "10 to 20 kilograms per month."

Kalamazoo and its effect on business

The Michigan Uber driver, 45-year-old Jason Brian Dalton, was charged with 16 counts at his arraignment, including six counts of murder and one count of attempted murder of a minor.

Despite the horrific violence Dalton is allegedly responsible for, local police confirmed he had no prior criminal record.

"If the person doesn't have a criminal record, then no background check is going to raise any flags," Uber's Durkosh said. "So, as that case has shown, past behavior may not accurately predict how people will behave in the future and that's where we think our technology features that we have in place can help ensure safety before, during, and after a ride in ways that other transportation options cannot."

Even with that technological advantage, Campbell said Uber could and should be doing more to spearhead improved safety features. "As a $60 billion company and a leader of the on-demand economy, I feel they should actually be leading the charge when it comes to these types of issues, instead of taking a backseat," Campbell said.

Despite safety concerns, Uber's growth has been spectacular. The company rose from a startup in 2009 to a platform revolutionizing the transportation industry in a short seven years.

Bloomberg Business reported Dec. 3 that the company is valued at $62.5 billion.

The University of Maryland's Bailey said it is difficult to measure how bad publicity will affect the company's worth because Uber is not yet publicly traded and its stock cannot be tracked.

"With privately-held companies, it's very difficult to ascertain kind of what their market capitalization is going to be at any given time," Bailey explained.

The future

While Uber has been mostly compliant with the wave of new legislation and in some cases has championed technological safety features, the glaring question of accountability persists for both investors and the public, according to Bailey.

Bailey said venture capitalists will look at the events in Michigan as a "stress test" for Uber's leadership and how they respond.

The long-term effects of the shooting in Michigan are still being felt now, with ride-booking legislation being passed in all but four states as of early April.

But for a company looking to become publicly traded some time in 2016 – the exact date remains unknown – Bailey said one question should be asked: "(Does the Kalamazoo shooting) somehow make the business model that Uber has completely unviable? Or is this a terrible tragedy, but ultimately not the responsibility of the platform like Uber?"

The public's perception of Uber's accountability, Bailey said, may "matter more than (the disclaimer) on their website."

> *"Today, we're living in the*
> *matchmaker economy. It is a bigger*
> *and more pervasive part of our lives*
> *than many imagine."*

This Economy Is Already a Big Part of Our Lives

David S. Evans and Richard Schmalensee

In the following viewpoint, David S. Evans and Richard Schmalensee argue that the idea for businesses to use new technology and innovations to surpass older businesses and render them obsolete is a tried-and-true strategy. The authors, David S. Evans and Richard Schmalensee, describe what they call the matchmaking industry and demonstrate how sites like Uber and Airbnb are prime examples of the businesses that make up this space. Evans is an economist, business adviser, and entrepreneur. Schmalensee is the Howard W. Johnson Professor of Management and Economics, Emeritus, at the Massachusetts Institute of Technology. Evans and Schmalensee co-authored Matchmakers: The New Economics of Multisided Platforms.

As you read, consider the following questions:

1. According to the authors, what is one of the oldest business models, and what is its purpose?
2. According to the authors, what are matchmakers, as the term applies to the sharing economy?
3. What reservation-booking service took years to develop, with its first viable cities being San Francisco and Chicago?

One of the oldest business models in the world is using new technology to trample traditional businesses, drive innovation, and create new and immense sources of value. Matchmakers, the subject of our new book, make it easy for two or more groups of customers, like drivers and riders in the case of Uber, to get together and do business. They operate platforms that make it easy and efficient for participants to connect and exchange value.

Unlike traditional businesses, they don't buy inputs, make stuff, and sell it. Instead, they recruit participants, and then sell each group of participants access to the other group of participants. The "participants" are the "inputs" that they use to produce the intermediation service they provide.

Today, we're living in the matchmaker economy. It is a bigger and more pervasive part of our lives than many imagine.

Three of the five most highly valued companies in the world — Apple, Google, and Microsoft — make much of their profits from connecting different groups, like developers and users in the case of Apple. So do seven of the most valuable unicorns — startups worth more than $1 billion in their latest funding round — such as Uber, Airbnb, and Flipkart. And then many other companies that have IPO'd in the last decade, like Visa, which connects cardholders and merchants, and Facebook, which connects friends, advertisers, and developers.

And it's not just these humongous companies. Westfield Malls operates shopping malls that help retailers and shoppers to get together. Then there are all the ad-supported media that troll for eyeballs so they can sell them to marketers.

In fact, if you think about, as a consumer and a worker, you probably use multiple matchmakers throughout your day, from the operating system on your phone, to an exchange for trading stock, to a dating app for finding a mate.

The firms that make up the gig economy and the sharing economy — the new darlings — are matchmakers too. Gig economy companies connect workers with consumers who need them, such as home care workers with families that need help, while sharing economy ones match up unused capacity, like automobiles, with people who want to rent them.

All matchmakers play by similar rules. But the rules are different than those for traditional firms.

Matchmakers have to solve the hardest problem in business — a critical mass of two or more groups of participants who value the service will sign on only if they can get access to the other groups of participants.

When OpenTable started it had trouble getting restaurants because it had few prospective diners, and had trouble getting prospective diners because it had few restaurants. It took OpenTable almost six years, and tens of millions of dollars of investment, to get enough restaurants and diners in just two cities — San Francisco and Chicago. Most platforms don't have such patient investors and simply implode during their failed attempts to reach critical mass, like the hundreds of B2B exchanges that died in the early 2000s.

Many successful matchmakers violate the rules of pricing that every beginning econ student learns. They sell their services to one group for less than cost, maybe even giving it away for free, or perhaps providing rewards. Google's indexing is invaluable to websites but the search giant doesn't charge any of them for the service. But even physical platforms often do this: Shopping

TWENTY-SOMETHING ECONOMICS

Uber, AirBnB and other companies that mine the so-called "sharing economy" continue to face legal and regulatory challenges, both in the United States and internationally.

At heart, these services use the Internet to scale up the sort of thing young people have done for ages. Going home for the weekend? Post a note on a dorm bulletin board offering to share gas and you'd likely get a ride. Coming into town for a big concert? With a few phone calls you could easily find a friend of a friend of a friend who would let you crash on his couch in return for a couple of six packs.

This is why Uber, Lyft and AirBnB strike such a chord with millennials. These three companies have the most mindshare, but there are many others on the rise: DogVacay (pet-sitting), RelayRides and GetAround (peer-to-peer car renting) and TaskRabbit (household chores and office help). They align perfectly with twenty-something economics, ever moreso today when your first "job" might be little more than an unpaid internship. Meanwhile, the platforms offer individuals a means of income in a changing job environment where conventional long-term employment opportunities are decreasing in favor automation and contract workers.

That's why, in the end, these services will win out, despite any short-term setbacks they encounter along the way from unimaginative local lawmakers with little else to do. They bring considerable ground-level muscle to a local economy. In the case of apartment- and ride-sharing, the easier it is to get buyers and sellers to and around your town, the more money they will spend in your town.

malls don't charge shoppers, for instance, and sometimes provide free entertainment.

Most significant matchmakers have something that no traditional business has — an elaborate governance system of laws, enforcement, and penalties to keep their participants in line. In

2009 a fifth of Facebook's employees were "policemen" patrolling the site for naughty stuff (we suspect the proportion is much lower today and the problem much greater). And there's a Google Jail, at least that's what its prisoners call it, where websites that game the search algorithm are sent to do time. And Apple hands down death sentences to apps that violate its rules or that it just doesn't like very much.

These matchmaker businesses are extending their tentacles all through the economy. Platforms are being erected on top of platforms that are being erected on top of platforms. Android, for example, is a platform for users, developers, and handset makers. Uber's platform for connecting drivers and passengers is built on top of Android (as well as the iPhone). And now Uber is building a platform on top of Uber that connects drivers, restaurants, and people who want a take-out meal.

The matchmaker business model is hardly new. Visa will turn 50 this year, the London Stock Exchange is more than 200 years old, and the Grand Bazaar in Istanbul more than 500. Today, though, matchmakers are turbocharged — powered by the cloud, broadband, microprocessors, software, and other modern technologies. Companies like Uber wouldn't exist, for example, without the development of mobile broadband, mobile software platforms, and the internet.

These turbocharged platforms, boosted by other turbocharged platforms, are marching around the globe, trampling both traditional businesses and older platforms. No business is safe in the path of this most recent gale of creative destruction.

In Kenya, the M-PESA mobile money platform is leapfrogging traditional banking and payment cards. Around 90% of adults use it to transfer money, and many use it for savings, borrowing, and other services.

Airbnb, which seems to have come out of nowhere, is challenging the global hotel industry. It has 1.5 million rooms, making it larger than Marriott.

Once impregnable platforms, like Microsoft Windows, are in decline. PC sales declined by 10% last year, reflecting the rapid move to mobile app platforms like Apple's iOS and Google's Android mobile operating systems and app stores.

Whether you are an investor, an entrepreneur, a worker at a traditional firm, or an established platform, you will need to learn what the oldest business model, newly turbocharged, means for you.

We bring to bear great optimism that the turbocharged matchmakers will power a gale of creative destruction that will sweep across the economy and produce great social value. But our views are tempered with realism that most who try this business model will fail miserably, after burning through mountains of cash. Some of the copycat "Uber for Something" companies will revolutionize industries, but most, like Shuddle, the ride-sharing service for kids, will close down, and become the "Uber for Nothing."

> "*Whether regulating peer-to-peer services is a good idea or not, these disputes need to be overcome if the sharing economy is to grow to the extent to which some have predicted it is capable.*"

The Sharing Economy Is Changing the Way Businesses Are Run

Laura French

In the following viewpoint, Laura French argues that the leading companies at the forefront of the peer-to-peer, or sharing economy, are changing how consumers perceive businesses and services and how companies offer said services. French explores how leaders, such as Airbnb, can—and do—impact their respective sectors. She addresses why consumers have responded, for the most part, so positively to these companies, and discusses the concerns and controversies that have also come into existence as a result of these emerging business models. French is a journalist with a focus on business and travel.

"Sharing Economy Shakes Up Traditional Business Models," by Laura French, *New Economy*, April 13, 2015. http://www.theneweconomy.com/business/the-sharing -economy-shakes-up-traditional-business-models. Reprinted by permission.

As you read, consider the following questions:

1. According to the author, what does venture capitalist and peer-to-peer investor Shervin Pishevar compare the importance of the movement of the sharing economy to, in the context of its impact?
2. What are some advantages that collaborative models have over traditional business models?
3. Which peer-to-peer business did Dean Baker, co-director of the Centre for Economic and Policy Research, say is "facilitating a bunch of rip-offs"?

The emergence of peer-to-peer sites such as Airbnb, Lyft and EatWith has been one of the more intriguing web developments of the last few years. These companies are overhauling the traditional concept of business versus consumer by enabling anyone to offer up their apartments, cars or culinary skills in return for cash.

What began as a niche sector, brushed aside by skeptics, has blossomed into a whole industry. There are over 9,000 companies in on the game, according to Mesh, a directory for the sharing economy. With everything from peer-to-peer money lending to lift sharing now available, consumers have a whole new world at their fingertips and it's sending shock waves across the globe.

PwC estimates five sharing economy sectors alone could generate a whopping $335bn in revenues between them by 2025. And, according to Nielsen, there's high demand for the collaborative economy – especially in emerging markets, where it's tipped to accelerate growth by giving consumers access to services they couldn't traditionally afford.

Advocates claim the sharing economy is creating a stronger sense of community while cutting back on waste. Among the supporters is Shervin Pishevar, venture capitalist and peer-to-peer investor: "This is a movement as important as when the web browser came out," he told *Forbes*. Time meanwhile ranked the sharing economy among its "10 Ideas that Will Change the World." The benefits are several, and could spell trouble for traditional businesses and economic models.

Rupturing tradition

The biggest change from traditional structures is the breakdown in the distinction between companies and customers, with peer-to-peer models giving consumers the opportunity to become businesspeople on a part-time, temporary and flexible level; whether by renting a pet-friendly room to a pooch-lover via DogVacay or offering up a neglected driveway via Parking Panda. Knocking down that consumer-producer wall is something social media has already, in part, achieved (with customers playing a more important role in marketing than ever before, for example) and the sharing economy seems a logical culmination of that gradual shift.

But it could mean bad news for traditional businesses that fail to adapt, according to Josh Goldman, Global Leader for Shopping Measurement at Nielsen. "These companies are creating new economic value and disrupting current established industry players", he says. Lisa Gansky, author of The Mesh: Why the Future of Business is Sharing, agrees: "There is a massive shift occurring and I believe all industries will be or are already being affected."

The impact of Uber on the traditional taxi industry is already evident: in San Francisco, for example, taxi usage has plummeted by around 65 percent, according to Kate Toran of the city's Municipal Transportation Agency (Engadget reported), while, in New York, shares in Medallion Financial Corp – which lends money to the famous yellow New York taxi operators – have tumbled almost 30 percent in a year as demand for the traditional taxis has plunged, according to Andrew Murstein.

Cheaper, more efficient markets

The potential impact of peer-to-peer accommodation sites such as Airbnb on the hospitality sector has meanwhile sparked further attention. In a report, researchers at Boston University estimated

SHIFT FROM RESOURCES TO ECOSYSTEM

The traditional view of competitive advantage has broken down. The traditional view was "big is beautiful." The more you own, the better you win. This led to the rise in popularity of vertical integration of business as well as to many mergers and acquisitions. Resources were how you competed.

Increasingly, resources are not the definition of scale anymore. Airbnb and Uber aren't multi-billion dollar businesses for the employees and resources they control in-house but for the ecosystem they succeed in attracting.

Ecosystems are the new scale and the new source of competitive advantage.

"From Social Media to the Sharing Economy: The Three Drivers of Business Disruption," platformthinkinglabs.com, 2015

that every 10 percent rise in Airbnb supply in Texas caused a 0.35 percent drop in monthly hotel revenue – equivalent to a fall in revenue of over 13 percent in Austin. They also found hotels had cut their room rates as a result of pressure from the lower peer-to-peer prices appealing to cash-conscious consumers.

As well as offering more affordable services to consumers, collaborative models are also arguably more resilient. While hotel supply is limited and any increase involves large-scale work, peer-to-peer accommodation is agile, its space limited only by the willingness of people to offer up their empty rooms. As Gansky points out, the world's largest hotel chain, Intercontinental, offers only 65 percent of Airbnb's current capacity. It's clearly working: according to the UK Economic Impact Study, Airbnb generated £502m in economic activity in the space of a year in the UK, and over 30 million people across the world have rented a room through the site.

"People are attracted to this peer-to-peer model for economic, environmental, lifestyle and personal reasons", says James McClure,

General Manager UK & Ireland at Airbnb. "More broadly speaking, the sharing economy has created markets out of things that wouldn't have been considered monetisable assets before." That means making efficient use of excess resources and minimising waste, especially relevant as consumers become evermore conscious of its damaging consequences. Goldman certainly agrees: "This model is creating more efficient markets, period," he says, adding it could help establish a better supply-demand equilibrium.

Hostile opposition

But there are several issues associated with this new model, and they're sparking widespread controversy. While Uber has provoked protests and bans across the world, peer-to-peer accommodation has kicked off a debate in New York, with public advocate Letitia James arguing: "Airbnb and the illegal hotel operators it enables are contributing to the affordable housing crisis."

Others have concluded the lax regulation of the sharing model could do more damage than good to economies. Dean Baker, Co-Director of the Centre for Economic and Policy Research, believes peer-to-peer businesses are providing a loophole for "a small number of people… to cheat the system." He wrote in The Guardian: "Insofar as Airbnb is allowing people to evade taxes and regulations, the company is not a net plus to the economy and society – it is simply facilitating a bunch of rip-offs." He argued Airbnb apartments should be taxed in the same way as hotels and that they, like Uber, should be made subject to the same safety standards as regular players.

But increased regulation and taxes are likely to mean higher prices for consumers, in part defeating the object of peer-to-peer companies designed to cut costs and move business away from the hands of overbearing authority. It's perhaps for that reason that a number of sharing economy advocates argue against regulating this new model; among them are senior research fellow Adam Thierer and his colleagues. "The key contribution of the sharing economy is that it has overcome market imperfections without recourse to traditional forms of regulation," they wrote in a paper. "Continued application of these outmoded regulatory regimes is likely to harm consumers."

Whether regulating peer-to-peer services is a good idea or not, these disputes need to be overcome if the sharing economy is to grow to the extent to which some have predicted it is capable. If it does – and it would seem a logical progression in a society characterised by constant connectivity – this model could eventually replace the traditional consumer-versus-provider structure. Key players must find a way to adapt effectively if they are to capitalise on its potential benefits.

> "*A lack of trust still casts its shadow over the more paranoid and less tech-savvy who may be reluctant to participate in libraries of things and the sharing economy in general, even with the added security of today.*"

If Millennials Are the Future, Then So Is the Sharing Economy

Lendogram

The following viewpoint argues that while there are still wrinkles to be ironed out, the sharing economy does indeed have staying power. Support for the concept of "own less, access more," is clear, and examples of how this is already happening are provided. The author notes that some of the specifics of the sharing economy are similar to the way millennials are used to doing business anyway; thus, as millennials age, the sharing economy will only become more pervasive. A case could also be made that this generation is less interested in acquisitions and more focused on social responsibility. Lendogram is a sharing platform.

"Why the Sharing Economy Is Here to Stay," Lendogram, Inc., March 19, 2016. Lendogram: http://lendogram.com/. Copyright © Lendogram.

As you read, consider the following questions:

1. According to the viewpoint, the sharing economy has a positive impact on Earth. How is this the case?
2. How can heating one's home be part of a sharing economy relationship?
3. What factors most contribute to the need for a sharing economy?

Lyft, Coursera, TaskRabbit, Airbnb, Zipcar? You may have seen these names, heard about them on the news, or used their services. These services are all manifestations of what's called the sharing economy (or peer-to-peer economy) in their own separate industries, and their popularity reflects a trend away from the more traditional consumerist style of buying from large corporations.

Wonder why? Well, since the crisis of 2008, the economy has become more precarious than ever, with household debt being steadily on the rise. This is especially true of the Millennials of the day (along with Generations X to a lesser, but still significant extent), who have also come to a realization that they could not live as their parents and grandparents did, what with the damage did to the Earth by the Industrial Revolution and beyond (Global warming, anyone?)

Thus, the response seems to be a sea change into a mindset of "own less, access more."

Adding on that with the increasing lack of income security, many more individuals have begun to rely on their own pre-existing resources, using their own ingenuity to further tap into things they have owned but not put to full use.

With internet penetration increasing daily worldwide, more people are able to use technology to mitigate the risks of sharing their own personal property. How?

Through the internet, and social media, we can use reputation checks or online records provided by service coordinators and platforms to ensure people are trustworthy, and the sharing economy thrives.

Indeed, it seems to be a win on multiple fronts. For one, you're tapping into resources you have but don't need to use all the time, by turning your very ownership into cold cash.

You've got a nice blue dress that you only wore once when your fifteenth cousin thrice removed got married? Rent it out to others, maybe. You get some of your cash back, and the person you rent it out to saves a pretty penny as they didn't have to buy a dress that they would only wear once!

Another thing is that the sharing economy, to put it simply, saves the Earth. With this, your assets might be used much more than if you weren't lending it to others as well. What's more is that you'll most certainly get much more mileage out of it than if you were using it alone, a point that hasn't been missed by the more environmentally conscious.

Let's look at another example, shall we?

In winter, you have to heat your whole house, and pay for utilities and upkeep throughout the year, but you're certainly not staying in there all the time, are you? In this, sharing a room produces less waste of gas, water, and electricity per person.

Your roommate and you may use more energy collectively – but less individually, so that means fewer greenhouse gas emissions!

To add on to that, if you have a car, even better! Sharing your car with your roommate spreads costs, as well as reduces emissions since you'll both be using one car instead of two individually again. Just a figure for you – car-sharing participants have been shown to reduce up to 40% of their individual emissions.

The third fact is when you share, you build stronger relationships and bonds with friends and people you share your stuff with. One more interaction in this busy world. Go out there – help your friends, form strong bonds, we don't live alone on our planet!

In our previous articles, we also mentioned several "Libraries of Things," which are perhaps the most innovative incarnation of the sharing economy. Indeed, the example of having to first learn how to use a tool, which you have borrowed, is one of many that serve as gateways to greater bonding within the community.

When you lend something to someone, you're going to want to know if you can trust them with your prized possessions – and what better way to get an impression of them than to interact with them in person? The sharing economy could be what we just need – a remedy to the individualistic and consumerist culture of late, and a chance to connect with others in an increasingly colder world.

But there is no doubt that there are some issues with the sharing economy. A lack of trust still casts its shadow over the more paranoid and less tech-savvy who may be reluctant to participate in libraries of things and the sharing economy in general, even with the added security of today.

Another point to notes is also the fact that such ideas, and companies have increasingly been subjected to increased taxes and regulations, inflating the costs for both consumer and business as traditional businesses or governments attempt to adapt to the appeal and popularity of the sharing economy for Millennials.

However, what is clear is that in the current climate, what with the rising costs of owning and maintaining assets such as houses and cars, as well as the increased jobs and services these provide for both consumer and worker – the sharing economy has found its niche and is here to stay.

> "A new economy in which we
> are increasingly masters of our
> jobs as well as our lives provides
> opportunities to work for things that
> matter to us and invent new forms of
> collaboration with fluid hierarchies."

The Sharing Economy Is Here to Stay, Sort of

Bernhard Resch

In the following viewpoint, Bernhard Resch argues that the economy of the future will lie somewhere in between the traditional economy and the sharing economy. Resch forecasts a future where machines take over much of the labor, leaving humans free to pursue entrepreneurship. Self-organization, where traditional employment hierarchies flatten out and workers collaborate in teams, will promote creativity. The cost, Resch argues, could be maintaining a separation of work life and private life. Resch is a researcher in Organizational Politics at the University of St.Gallen, in Switzerland, with a focus on self-organized work practices—that is, managing without a caste of managers.

As you read, consider the following questions:

1. What percentage of the US workforce is projected to freelance in 2020, as compared to 2006 and 2015?
2. Which presidential candidate suggested that the gig economy was unhealthy, according to the author?
3. What does the author mean when he refers to "platform capitalism?"

Uber suffered a legal blow this week when a California judge granted class action status to a lawsuit claiming the car-hailing service treats its drivers like employees, without providing the necessary benefits.

Up to 160,000 Uber chauffeurs are now eligible to join the case of three drivers demanding the company pay for health insurance and expenses such as mileage. Some say a ruling against the company could doom the business model of the on-demand or "sharing" economy that Uber, Upwork and TaskRabbit represent.

Whatever the outcome, it's unlikely to reverse the most radical reinvention of work since the rise of industrialization – a massive shift toward self-employment typified by on-demand service apps and enabled by technology. That's because it's not a trend driven solely by these tech companies.

Workers themselves, especially millennials, are increasingly unwilling to accept traditional roles as cogs in the corporate machinery being told what to do. Today, 34% of the US workforce freelances, a figure that is estimated to reach 50% by 2020. That's up from the 31% estimated by the Government Accountability Office in a 2006 study.

Rise of the gig-based economy

In place of the traditional notion of long-term employment and the benefits that came with it, app-based platforms have given birth to the gig-based economy, in which workers create a living through a patchwork of contract jobs.

Uber and Lyft connect drivers to riders. TaskRabbit helps someone who wants to remodel a kitchen or fix a broken pipe find a nearby worker with the right skills. Airbnb turns everyone into hotel proprietors, offering their rooms and flats to strangers from anywhere.

Thus far, the industries where this transformation has occurred have been fairly low-skilled, but that's changing. Start-ups Medicast, Axiom and Eden McCallum are now targeting doctors, legal workers and consultants for short-term contract-based work.

A 2013 study estimated that almost half of US jobs are at risk of being replaced by a computer within 15 years, signaling most of us may not have a choice but to accept a more tenuous future.

The economic term referring to this transformation of how goods and services are produced is "platform capitalism," in which an app and the engineering behind it bring together customers in neat novel economic ecosystems, cutting out traditional companies.

But is the rise of the gig economy a bad thing, as Democratic front-runner Hillary Clinton suggested in July when she promised to "crack down on bosses misclassifying workers as contractors"?

While some contend this sweeping change augurs a future of job insecurity, impermanence and inequality, others see it as the culmination of a utopia in which machines will do most of the labor and our workweeks will be short, giving us all more time for leisure and creativity.

My recent research into self-organized work practices suggests the truth lies somewhere in between. Traditional hierarchies provide a certain security, but they also curb creativity. A new economy in which we are increasingly masters of our jobs as well as our lives provides opportunities to work for things that matter to us and invent new forms of collaboration with fluid hierarchies.

Sharing into the abyss?

Critics such as essayist Evgeny Morozov or the philosopher Byung-Chul Han highlight the dark side of this "sharing economy."

Instead of a collaborative commons, they envision the commercialization of intimate life. In this view, the likes of Uber and Airbnb are perverting the initial collaborative nature of their business models – car-sharing and couch-surfing – adding a price and transforming them from shared goods into commercial products. The unspoken assumption is that you have the choice between renting and owning, but "renting" will be the default option for the majority.

Idealists take another tack. Part of the on-demand promise is that technology makes it easier to share not only cultural products but also cars, houses, tools or even renewable energy. Add increasing automation to the picture and it invokes a society in which work is no longer the focus. Instead, people spend more of their time in creative and leisurely activities. Less drudge, more time to think.

The "New Work movement," formed by philosopher Frithjof Bergmann in the late 1980s, envisioned such a future, while economist and social theorist Jeremy Rifkin imagines consumers and producers becoming one and the same: prosumers.

From self-employment to self-organization

Both of these extremes seem to miss the mark. In my view, the most decisive development underlying this discussion is the need for worker self-organization as the artificial wall between work and life dissolves.

My recent work has involved studying how the relationship between managers and workers has evolved, from traditional structures that are top-down, with employees doing what they're told, to newer ones that boast self-managing teams with managers counseling them or even the complete abolition of formal hierarchies of rank.

While hierarchy guarantees a certain security and offers a lot of stability, its absence frees us to work more creatively and collaboratively. When we're our own boss we bear more responsibility, but also more reward.

And as we increasingly self-organize alongside others, people start to experiment in various ways, from peer to peer and open source projects to social entrepreneurship initiatives, bartering circles and new forms of lending.

The toughest tension for workers will be how best to balance private and work-related demands as they are increasingly interwoven.

Avoiding the pitfalls of platform capitalism

Another risk is that we will become walled in by the platform capitalism being built by Uber and TaskRabbit but also Google, Amazon and Apple, in which companies control their respective ecosystems. Thus, our livelihoods remain dependent on them, like in the old model, just without the benefits workers have fought for many decades.

In his recent book "Postcapitalism," Paul Mason eloquently puts it like this: "the main contradiction today is between the possibility of free, abundant goods and information; and a system of monopolies, banks and governments trying to keep things private, scarce and commercial."

To avoid this fate, it's essential to create sharing and on-demand platforms that follow a non-market rationale, such as through open source technologies and nonprofit foundations, to avoid profit overriding all other considerations. The development of the operating system Linux and web browser Firefox are examples of the possibility and merits of these models.

Between hell and heaven

Millennials grew up in the midst of the birth of a new human age, with all the world's knowledge at their fingertips. As they take over the workforce, the traditional hierarchies that have long dictated work will continue to crumble.

Socialized into the participatory world of the web, millennials prefer to self-organize in a networked way using readily available communication technology, without bosses dictating goals and deadlines.

But this doesn't mean we'll all be contractors. Frederic Laloux and Gary Hamel have shown in their impressive research that a surprisingly broad range of companies have already acknowledged these realities. Amazon-owned online shoe retailer Zappos, computer game designer Valve and tomato-processor Morning Star, for example, have all abolished permanent managers and handed their responsibilities over to self-managing teams. Without job titles, team members flexibly adapt their roles as needed.

Mastering this new way of working takes us through different networks and identities and requires the capacity to organize oneself and others as well as to adapt to fluid hierarchies.

As such, it may be the the fulfillment of Peter Drucker's organizational vision:

> … in which every man sees himself as a "manager" and accepts for himself the full burden of what is basically managerial responsibility: responsibility for his own job and work group, for his contribution to the performance and results of the entire organization, and for the social tasks of the work community.

Periodical and Internet Sources Bibliography

The following articles have been selected to supplement the diverse views presented in this chapter.

Yokai Benkler, "Sharing Nicely": On Shareable Goods and the Emergence of Sharing as a Modality of Economic Production, Yale Law School Legal Scholarship Repository, January 1, 2004. http://digitalcommons.law.yale.edu/cgi/viewcontent .cgi?article=4058&context=fss_papers.

Damien Demailly and Anne-Sophie Novel, "The Sharing Economy: Make it Sustainable," The Institute for Sustainable Development and International Relations. http://www.iddri.org/Publications /Economie-du-partage-enjeux-et-opportunites-pour-la -transition-ecologique.

Sarah Kessler, "The Sharing Economy Is Dead and We Killed It," *Fast Company*, September 14, 2015. https://www.fastcompany .com/3050775/the-sharing-economy-is-dead-and-we-killed-it.

Ryan Lawler, "Airbnb Tops 10 Million Guest Stays Since Launch, Now Has 550,000 Properties Listed Worldwide," techcrunch.com, December 19, 2013. https://techcrunch.com/2013/12/19/airbnb -10m/.

Jan Lee, "Is the Sharing Economy Innately Sustainable?," TriplePundit.com, January 23, 2013. http://www.triplepundit .com/special/rise-of-the-sharing-economy/sharing-economy -innately-sustainable/.

Ryan Mac, "Under 30 Tech CEOs Emphasize Trust as Key to the Sharing Economy," *Forbes,* October 17, 2016. http://www.forbes .com/sites/ryanmac/2016/10/17/under-30-tech-ceos-emphasize -trust-as-key-to-the-sharing-economy/#1e58c16d4630.

Kurt Matzler, Victoria Veider, and Wolfgang Kathan, "Adapting to the Sharing Economy," *MIT Sloan Management Review*, Winter 2015. http://sloanreview.mit.edu/article/adapting-to-the-sharing -economy/.

Molly McCluskey, "Sharing Is Declaring: How the Peer-to-Peer Economy Affects Your Taxes," *U.S. News & World Report*, February 9, 2015. http://money.usnews.com/money/personal

-finance/articles/2015/02/19/sharing-is-declaring-how-the-peer
-to-peer-economy-affects-your-taxes.

Evie Nagy, "Uber Is a Verb," Fast Company, September 9, 2015.
https://www.fastcompany.com/3050660/most-creative-people
/uber-is-a-verb.

George Ritzer, "Prosumption: Evolution, Revolution, or Eternal
Return of the Same?," *Journal of Consumer Culture*,
November 6, 2013. http://journals.sagepub.com/doi
/abs/10.1177/1469540513509641.

Alex Stephany, "Beyond Uber and Airbnb: The Future of the Sharing
Economy," *Los Angeles Times*, May 19, 2014. http://www.latimes
.com/opinion/opinion-la/la-ol-sharing-economy-20140519-story
.html.

Matthew Yeomans, "Why the Sharing Economy Has a Sustainability
Problem," Inc.com http://www.inc.com/matthew-yeomans/why
-the-sharing-economy-has-a-sustainability-problem.html.

Tx Zhuo, "The Sharing Economy Isn't a Niche. It's the Future of
Market Capitalism," *Entrepreneur*, November 24, 2015. https://
www.entrepreneur.com/article/253070.

For Further Discussion

Chapter 1

1. Benita Matofska lays out ten building blocks, which he describes as the foundations of the sharing economy. Which three do you think are most important, and why?
2. Frank Pasquale and Siva Vaidhyanathan argue that the efforts behind corporate nullification ultimately have negative effects on society. What are their strongest points about this?
3. Kristofer Erickson offers several interpretations of sharing and the sharing economy. Which one do you think is the strongest? How do you define these concepts?

Chapter 2

1. Georgios Petropoulos discusses conflicts and concerns between the taxi industry and the rise of Uber's prevalence. Which of the arguments made in this article are strongest? Why?
2. Brishen Rogers says, "Uber may become the Myspace or Netscape of ride sharing—that is, a pioneer that could not maintain its market position." What is some evidence that supports this argument?
3. According to Stephen King, the new wave of internet businesses simply do not fit into the mold of traditional models. What are some points to support this argument?

Chapter 3

1. What do you think is Robin Chase's strongest point about the peer-to-peer economy and how governments should be responding? What are some ways to tackle this, in your opinion?

2. How did Chris Martin arrive at his forecasts, since as he states the current research is scant? Do you think his analysis is legitimate?

3. Duncan McCann questions whether the new economy can sustain what he calls "good jobs." Do you think it can? Why or why not?

Chapter 4

1. Dan Russo and Maggie DeBlasis cover the safety concerns that come with the use of Uber and similar businesses. What do you believe are the biggest safety issues on this front, and what can be done to help move them in the right direction?

2. Laura French points out some of the changes that need to take place if the sharing economy is to survive. What are her strongest suggestions, and why? And what additional suggestions do you have? Discuss what makes those ideas strong as well.

3. Which of the employment forecasts that Bernhard Resch outlines seem the most likely to come true? Why? Can you think of alternative outcomes?

Organizations to Contact

The editors have compiled the following list of organizations concerned with the issues debated in this book. The descriptions are derived from materials provided by the organizations. All have publications or information available for interested readers. The list was compiled on the date of publication of the present volume; the information provided here may change. Be aware that many organizations take several weeks or longer to respond to inquiries, so allow as much time as possible.

Better Business Bureau
Council of Better Business Bureaus, 3033 Wilson Blvd.,
Suite 600, Arlington, VA 22201
703-276-0100
Website: http://www.bbb.org

For more than 100 years, Better Business Bureau has been helping people find businesses, brands, and charities they can trust. In 2015, people turned to BBB more than 172 million times for BBB Business Profiles on more than 5.3 million businesses and Charity Reports on 11,000 charities, all available for free at bbb.org. The Council of Better Business Bureaus is the umbrella organization for the local, independent BBBs in the United States, Canada, and Mexico, as well as home to its national and international programs on dispute resolution, advertising review, and industry self-regulation.

Edward Lowe Foundation
58220 Decatur Road, Cassopolis, MI 49031
800-232-LOWE
Website: http://www.edwardlowe.org

The Edward Lowe Foundation was established by Ed and Darlene Lowe in 1985. In contrast to most US foundations, which are grant-giving entities, this is an operating foundation that funds its own programs. The foundation's entrepreneurship initiatives are focused on second-stage companies—growth-oriented firms that have moved beyond startup but haven't yet reached maturity. Their peer learning, leadership education, and strategic information programs are geared to help these companies continue growing. They also educate communities about the challenges second-stagers face and how to work with them.

Entrepreneurs' Organization

500 Montgomery Street, Suite 700, Alexandria,VA 22314
703-519-6700
Website: http://www.eonetwork.org

With global and local chapters, EO helps leading entrepreneurs learn and grow through peer-to-peer learning, once-in-a-lifetime experiences, and connections to experts.

National Business Education Association

nbea@nbea.org
Website: http//www.nbea.org

The National Business Education Association (NBEA) is the nation's leading professional organization devoted exclusively to serving individuals and groups engaged in instruction, administration, research, and dissemination of information for and about business. NBEA is the leading association devoted to the recognition that business education competencies are essential for all individuals in today's fast-changing society.

New York City Taxi and Limousine Commission

33 Beaver Street, New York, NY 10004
718-391-5501
Website: http://www.nyc.gov

The mission of the Taxi and Limousine Commission is to ensure that New Yorkers and visitors to the City have access to taxicabs, car services, and commuter van services that are safe, efficient, sufficiently plentiful, and provide a good passenger experience.

They understand that private transportation services are an essential component of the City's transit network, alongside publicly operated mass transit. They believe both in the power of market forces to ensure that supply meets demand, and in the need for intelligent regulation to set the rules of competition, ensure safety, provide transparency to market participants, and reduce unwanted externalities such as pollution.

Securities and Exchange Commission

SEC Headquarters, 100 F Street, NE, Washington, DC 20549
202-942-8088
Website: http://www.sec.gov

The mission of the SEC is to protect investors; maintain fair, orderly, and efficient markets; and facilitate capital formation. The SEC strives to promote a market environment that is worthy of the public's trust.

Bibliography of Books

Beth Buczynski. *Sharing Is Good: How to Save Money, Time and Resources through Collaborative Consumption*. New York, NY: New Society Publishers. 2013.

Glenn Carter. *Secrets of the Sharing Economy*. CreateSpace Independent Publishing Platform. 2015.

Robin Chase. *Peers Inc: How People and Platforms Are Inventing the Collaborative Economy and Reinventing Capitalism*. New York, NY: Public Affairs. 2015.

Edited by Cary Coglianese, Contributions by Jim Ellis *Achieving Regulatory Excellence*. Washington, DC: Brookings Institution Press. 2016.

Lisa Gansky. *The Mesh: Why the Future of Business Is Sharing*. New York, NY: Portfolio, 2012.

Steven Hill. *Raw Deal: How the "Uber Economy" and Runaway Capitalism Are Screwing American Workers*. New York, NY: St. Martin's Press. 2015.

Billee Howard. *We-Commerce: How to Create, Collaborate, and Succeed in the Sharing Economy*. New York, NY: TarcherPerigree. 2015.

Bryan J. Kramer. *Shareology: How Sharing Is Powering the Human Economy*. New York, NY: Morgan James Publishing. 2015.

Jared Meyer. *Uber-Positive: Why Americans Love the Sharing Economy*. New York, NY: Encounter Intelligence Series, Encounter Books. 2016.

Janelle Orsi. *Practicing Law in the Sharing Economy: Helping People Build Cooperatives, Social Enterprise, and Local Sustainable Economies*. Chicago, IL: American Bar Association. 2013.

Catherine E. Rudder and A. Lee Fritschler. *Public Policymaking by Private Organizations*. Washington, DC: Brookings Institution Press. 2016.

Mike Scantlebury and Jane Wood. *Living in the Sharing Economy*. Lulu.com. 2014.

Tom Slee, *What's Yours Is Mine*. New York, NY: OR Books. 2016.

Timothy Sprinkle. *Screw the Valley: A Coast-to-Coast Tour of America's New Tech Startup Culture: New York, Boulder, Austin, Raleigh, Detroit, Las Vegas, Kansas City*. Dallas, TX: BenBella Books. 2015.

Alex Stephany. *The Business of Sharing: Making It in the New Sharing Economy*. New York, NY: Palgrave Macmillan. 2015.

Arun Sundararajan. *The Sharing Economy: The End of Employment and the Rise of Crowd-Based Capitalism*. Cambridge, MA: MIT Press Ltd, US. 2016.

Index

.